3-Minute Motivators

More than 100 simple ways to reach, teach, and achieve more than you ever imagined

Kathy Paterson

Pembroke Publishers Limited

Pembroke Publishers
538 Hood Road
Markham, Ontario, Canada L3R 3K9
www.pembrokepublishers.com

Distributed in the U.S. by Stenhouse Publishers
480 Congress Street
Portland, ME 04101
www.stenhouse.com

We acknowledge the financial support of the Government of Canada through the Book
Publishing Industry Development Program (BPIDP) for our publishing activities.

We acknowledge the Government of Ontario through the Ontario Media Development
Corporation's Ontario Book Initiative.

Library and Archives Canada Cataloguing in Publication

Paterson, Kathy,
    3-minute motivators : more than 100 simple ways to reach, teach, and
achieve more than you ever imagined / Kathy Paterson.

Includes index.
ISBN 978-1-55138-215-9

1. Teaching. 2. Motivation in education. 1. Enseignement. 2. Motivation en éducation.
I. Title. II. Title: Three minute motivators.

LB1025.3.P3853 2007   371.102   C2007-904159-0

Editor: Kat Mototsune
Cover Design: John Zehethofer
Typesetting: Jay Tee Graphics Ltd.

Mixed Sources
Product group from well-managed
forests, and other controlled sources
www.fsc.org Cert no. SW-COC-002358
© 1996 Forest Stewardship Council
FSC

Printed and bound in Canada
9 8 7 6 5 4

Contents

Introduction: A Touch of Magic

This is a book about magic! As every teacher knows, the best teaching involves an element of magic—in the persona of the instructor, the presentation of curriculum, or the motivation of the students. Without a touch of magic, teaching is mundane, students are uninspired, lessons are less powerful and more forgettable. Consider the following:

Before…
The students are restless. As Miss Black, the teacher, attempts to walk them through the steps for solving the problem, she notes that several are whispering, a couple are daydreaming, another is engaged in annoying the person in front, and most have that familiar vacant "no-one-home" stare. The brilliant spring sun shining through the window is definitely much more engaging than the teacher is. She stops talking to see if they will refocus; most don't even seem to notice that she has stopped her presentation.

Teachers will recognize this scenario. It's safe to say that most, if not all, have experienced similar situations and probably are, with increasing frequency, struggling with UUSS—Unmotivated/Unfocused Student Syndrome.

Why? What is making it so difficult for us to reach/teach our students? Is there some way to wake them up, to turn them on, to keep them involved and stimulated? Is there a secret method for competing with the highly technological worlds of our students, where they are bombarded with sensual stimuli on a daily basis?

Yes, I think there is! Consider this "after" image:

After…
Miss Black shakes her tambourine loudly. All eyes immediately turn to her and talking ceases. Her pre-established and reinforced cue has done its job well. Then she says quietly, "I can see I have lost most of you. Time for a refocuser! A little game…" The students are interested. They are familiar with refocusers and enjoy these brief interjections. "Turn to a neighbor," Miss Black continues. "Let's play Shake It!" (see page 49). Immediately the students are completely engaged in the activity, laughing, talking, and attempting to "shake" the number called by the teacher. After about one minute, Miss Black interrupts the activity by once more shaking the tambourine. "Thanks for stopping on the cue," she says sincerely. "Now that we've shaken out a bit of that excess energy, it's time to return to the problem I was talking to you about…" The students, refocused, return to the task. This time all eyes are on the teacher.

The teacher in this scenario used a little magic to refocus her group; she provided an escape for excess energy then efficiently drew the students back into her lesson. She used a 3-Minute Motivator. 3-Minute Motivators are simple activities that can be use with any grade, and with any diversity found in the classroom. I have even experienced great success using them with university students and adults at conventions and workshops.

3-Minute Motivators is a collection of these concise activities that can be carried out *at* the desks, *beside* the desks, or *near* the desks, with minimum or no teacher preparation, making use of few props other than the occasional paper and pencil. The actions are designed to involve all the students in interesting, highly motivating ways, for approximately three minutes, then to refocus them on the task at hand. Magic!

But why are such activities necessary? Shouldn't students have intrinsic motivation to learn? Shouldn't they want to grow intellectually? Don't they appreciate the personal need for development as human beings? I believe the answer to each question is "yes"; unfortunately, there are so many high-level, sense-bombarding, almost mind-numbing distractions in today's society that classroom learning can appear boring, inauthentic, and monotonous.

Consider the students' world. How can children be excited and motivated by what they often see as dreary and lacklustre curriculum, when they are inundated with MP3 players, cell phones, handheld game systems, and countless highly technological video games? How can they pay attention to a lesson when they are tempted daily by a wealth of stimulating information at their fingertips via the Internet? How can they sustain single-mindedness for seatwork when they are eager to get back to their camera/game/cell phone and home entertainment system?

It takes a touch of magic to keep students inspired and focused today. *3-Minute Motivators* attempts to address this issue by offering a wealth of motivating activities ready for instant use in any classroom. In addition, most of these motivators can be readily adapted to be used as anticipatory sets for a wide variety of lessons. Once you have experimented with a few of them, I think you will agree that they are, indeed, magical. Use them with an open mind; have fun!

3-Minute Motivators in Your Classroom

You will find many uses for the 3-Minute Motivators. Not all of them are unique; some of them may already be familiar to teachers. Others may be new ways to look at common activities. Use them with passion and a sense of humor as often as needed, and enjoy the positive benefits they bring to the classroom.

More Than Just Motivation

What exactly *is* a 3-Minute Motivator? It is a quick activity, directed by the teacher, in which students *want* to participate because they see it as a game, appreciating the inherent play and fun. Whether it involves competition, cooperation, or individual thought or action, it provides a much-needed break from an undertaking that has lost the students' interest, and then re-concentrates attention and energy back to the teaching/learning task at hand. This re-concentration serves to point the students in the right direction once again—to refocus their attention; hence I often refer to these interventions as *refocusers*, a term that students quickly learn and accept.

Why use a 3-Minute Motivator?

- To give students a positive break
- To give the teacher a positive break; teachers need breaks too, and these speedy, easy-to-use activities help.
- To refocus flagging attentions
- To remove excess energy
- To wake up lethargic minds
- To introduce a lesson; most of the activities can have an anticipatory set function.
- To reward good behavior; they are fun, after all!

As with any good teaching strategies, 3-Minute Motivators all fall within a fairly consistent set of guidelines. For example, they can be satisfactorily completed within a brief amount of time. Your use of 3-Minute Motivators will be controlled by certain other basic understandings:

- There is no wrong answer.
- Variety is good and is encouraged.
- All responses are celebrated.
- Private space, both physical and emotional, is always respected.

Teachers will recognize these as important truths for all teaching, but they need to be reaffirmed with refocusers as they do with other classroom activities.

Inherent Learning

Although 3-Minute Motivators work to refocus attentions, they also have inherent learning that, if the teacher chooses, can be elaborated upon. For example, the

Shake It! motivator (page 49) indirectly teaches and reinforces the concepts of probability and luck, while providing practice in mentally adding and subtracting, and in cooperating with peers. Every one of the refocusers can be broken down into probable learning and a possible focus *specific* to the curriculum, if so desired.

Let's look at Interactive Words (page 63) as an example. Here are just a few areas (there are many more) where this refocuser fits conveniently into a Language Arts program of studies at the Grade 3 level:

- Experiment with rearranging of material
- Use organizational skills to clarify meaning
- Use a variety of strategies for comprehension
- Extend sight vocabulary
- Apply knowledge of graphophonic cueing systems
- Apply word analysis strategies
- Associate sounds with increasing number of vowel combinations
- Apply structural analysis cues
- Explain relationships among letters in words
- Experiment with words
- Use phonics knowledge
- Speak and read with fluency, rhythm, pace
- Work cooperatively with others

Another way to use these specific motivators is as quick anticipatory sets for appropriate lessons. For example, Shake It! (page 49) could be used prior to a math class on addition, subtraction, or even fractions. Synonym Sense (page 80) might make a motivating anticipatory set for a Language Arts class on descriptive writing.

Now consider the same motivator from the point of view of students' inherent learning. While participating in Interactive Words, it is quite possible that many, if not all, of them would learn, quite naturally, the following:

- Words can be broken into parts.
- Letters all have unique sounds.
- Letter combinations have unique sounds.
- Big words often contain smaller words within them.
- Chanting words one letter at a time helps with spelling.
- Chanting with peers is a rewarding activity.

No doubt this same motivator could be examined successfully from the standpoint of the other core subject curricula as well. It is always good for teachers to know that what they are doing is not only highly motivating, but also is viable as far as teaching to the existing program of studies and incidental inherent learning.

Choosing a 3-Minute Motivator

Teachers can simply select an activity at random. For example, the Math class is "lost"—a 3-Minute Motivator is called for! The book opens to Word Tennis (page 81) and within a couple of minutes all students are busily tossing Math vocabulary back and forth between partners. A random choice but effective nonetheless.

Using this book is primarily a matter of choosing the best activity for any given moment and situation.

All teachers are fully aware of the importance of purpose when teaching. It is mandatory for a teacher—and even students—to know *why* something is being presented, reviewed, or taught. The same goes for using 3-Minute Motivators. Quickly deciding *why* one of them is about to be used can be a determining factor in selecting the best motivator. Is it just to refocus the students, or is another purpose to be met at the same time? Certainly the single act of refocusing students so that a lesson can begin or be continued is significant, and often sufficient; however, teachers usually want to meet as many requirements as possible with every classroom action.

With this in mind, the question arises: "Aren't all 3-Minute Motivators mainly designed to motivate?" Yes, but student distractions can present as restlessness, hyperactivity, fatigue, or apathy (to name a few). Moreover, many other variables come into play, such as time of day or week, subject being interrupted by the motivator, or teacher stance (i.e. current level of patience, acceptance, or frustration). Therefore, the choice of the best motivator becomes a bit more difficult.

Skim or scan the activities described in the different sections, highlight or tab the ones you find most interesting or most appropriate for your group, then keep the book readily available for instant access.

Teachers may, for example, be faced with students who are vacant and sleepy-looking; they might choose a motivator that will "wake them up" and provide the jolt of energy necessary to complete the assignment or lesson. Or a teacher might want to get students communicating prior to a Social Studies discussion and, perhaps because it is Friday afternoon and it's raining outside, the children are noisy, out-of-seat, and restless—in this case a motivator that involves sitting and speaking may be what is required.

To simplify the process of finding the right motivator for any situation, the activities have been organized into groups, and then further specified as types. For example, the At Your Desks group of motivators all require the minimum of physical movement and are divided into two types: Calm Down motivators involve being still and thinking (see page 19); Pencil and Paper activities have the students using these tools to complete the tasks (see page 29). For descriptions of the different types of motivators in the Up and At 'Em group of more action-oriented activities see page 38 for the Get Moving type, page 49 for the Act, Don't Speak type, and page 57 for the Words and Movement type. 3-Minute Motivators in the Let's Communicate group are divided into types that focus on Single Words and Sounds (page 62), Conversation (page 69), and Brainstorm (page 77). Finally, the last group of motivators can be used as extended activities that go Beyond the Three-Minute Mark (page 85)

When choosing a 3-Minute Motivator out of the 123 in this book, your best tool may be the 3-Minute Motivators at a Glance table on pages 11–13. A quick scan of the table will give you an idea of the nature of each motivator and any particular subjects it might be most useful to address.

Suggested Subject(s)

Many of the activities are more appropriate for one subject or another, so Subject(s) have been listed both in the 3-Minute Motivators at a Glance table (pages 11–13) and on each activity. While not intended to limit use of any specific motivator to the subject(s) suggested, the labels indicate the subject most likely addressed.

Many motivators have no specific subject affinity, or have a cross-curricular nature, indicated by the Subject label *Any*.

If, for example, the teacher wants to use a motivator during a Science lesson, and doesn't want students to lose the "Science" train of thought, a logical choice might be an activity with a *Science* label attached. Keep in mind, however, that any motivator can be used with, or during, any subject.

Noteworthy is the fact that all the activities involve some sort of communication, and all address *most* strands of the Language Arts curriculum.

Number of Students

Note also that the motivators are categorized as *Individual, Partners, Small Group,* or *Whole Class,* allowing teachers to narrow their choices. If students are being too social, for example, perhaps a motivator listed as *Individual* would be more effective than one that involves partner or small-group work.

When having students find partners or form small groups, it is often most expedient to have "neighbors," or students adjacent to each other, work together. Teachers may wish to mix things up by suggesting that students pair with someone other than the person with whom they usually work. Heterogeneous mixing is often advantageous, and the low-risk nature of these activities lends itself to such combinations.

3-Minute Motivators that are performed alone by each student, without conferring in any way with peers, are listed as *Individual*. Some activities have individual students adding to, being a part of, or helping to complete a task that involves the whole class; these motivators are labelled *Individual as part of Whole Class*. 3-Minute Motivators that have students working in pairs are listed as *Partners*. In some instances, partners work together to compete with the whole class, challenging other pairs in a competitive way; these activities are labelled *Partners as part of Whole Class*.

Keep in mind that these labels are just suggestions; most motivators can be altered to work individually or otherwise.

Props

A part of your choice of activity may be whether or not you need to acquire and distribute materials to use.

A few of the 3-Minute Motivators suggest the use of music props. The music usually referred to is of the slow, calming genre often found on yoga music, relaxation, or environmental CDs. Even some classical music will work. The key is to keep the music soft and soothing, so it operates in the background to set mood. Be sure the music has no lyrics. Please note, however, that with the exception of Hearing Colors (page 21), all motivators will work well without music.

Other props may be as simple as pencil and paper, a coin, or flash cards. Prop labels have been used to simplify your choice. In a hurry? Avoid an activity with a prop.

Extending the Activities

When using an Extended Debrief at the end of the 3-Minute Motivator, say, "Remember what you did (thought, visualized, said, etc.) and we'll come back to that after we finish our lesson."

Consider the Debrief and Showcase sections provided for some activities. A note to Debrief means that the activity is a good one for a brief follow-up discussion. To keep within the 3-Minute part of the definition (necessary if lesson flow is to be maintained), a 60-second "discuss with a neighbor" is suggested.

If the motivator has an Extended Debrief outlined, this indicates an activity that will work well with a longer, more in-depth discussion, and perhaps lead to writing (e.g., journal reflection, story starter, sequenced directions) or representation (e.g., creating a poster or visual, puppet presentation, drama skit). I have listed proposals for some of these Extended Debriefs; however, these are merely suggestions. No one knows your class better than you, and your ideas for Extended Debriefs are limitless.

Some 3-Minute Motivators include suggestions for Showcase. This indicates that this particular activity could be shared with peers. The showcase can be as simple as a 30-second time for students to show the rest of the class the products of their activity, to an elaborate sharing with other classes and parents, as part of an open house or concert. Often children enjoy showing off something they feel is cool or amusing, so why not encourage their natural desire to let others see what they have done?

Some of the 3-Minute Motivators make use of lists of ideas, word combinations, situations, themes, etc. It is often difficult to generate instant inventories on the spur of the moment; therefore, I came to depend on lists that I kept on file cards in a box on my desk. Teachers may wish to transfer some of the more commonly used lists to cards for themselves.

The time allowed for a Showcase should be within the three-minute proscription. We're talking about a quick, snappy sharing here. Not all students will be able to showcase every time, so you will need to be aware of turn-taking and equal opportunity. If everyone wants to showcase a particular activity, the best approach would be to point out that you will share when the interrupted lesson has been completed, thereby avoid losing the flow of the lesson.

3-Minute Motivators at a Glance

	Motivator	Page	Suggested Subject(s)
At Your Desks: Calm Down			
1	Belly Breathing	20	Health & Wellness
2	Collecting Clouds	20	Science
3	Hearing Colors	21	Art; Health & Wellness
4	Magic Carpet	21	Language Arts; Art
5	Imagine This	22	Any
6	Time Machine	23	Science
7	Chocolate & Bricks	24	Any, especially Health & Wellness
8	Grounding Exercise	25	Any; Use pre-exam
9	Hug-a-Tree	25	Science; Health & Wellness
10	Silent Scream	26	Health & Wellness; Social Studies
11	Absolutely Nothing!	26	Any
12	The Key	27	Language Arts
13	Lift Off!	27	Science
14	Zen Garden	28	Art; Health & Wellness
15	Telescope	28	Science
At Your Desks: Pencil and Paper			
16	Box Me In	29	Any
17	Circles & Squares	30	Science; Math
18	O's and X's	30	Any
19	Letter Scramble	30	Language Arts
20	4-Word Lotto	31	Any as source of words
21	Never-ending Line	31	Art; Math; Science
22	Draw My Words	31	Art; Science; Language Arts
23	Number Madness	32	Math

	Motivator	Page	Suggested Subject(s)
24	Written Rumor	33	Language Arts
25	Shared-Pen Stories	33	Language Arts
26	Zoom-Out	34	Science
27	Scrabble Scramble	35	Language Arts; Any as source of theme
28	Add-Ons	35	Any
29	Blind Draw	36	Health & Wellness; Language Arts; Social Studies
30	Snowglobe Drawings	36	Any
31	Mirror Images	37	Language Arts; Science; Math
Up and At 'Em: Get Moving			
32	Open–Shut–Shake	38	Any; especially for fine motor control
33	Puppet Master	39	Language Arts; Social Studies
34	The Big Yawn	39	Any
35	Glass Blower	40	Science; Social Studies
36	Levitating Arms	40	Science
37	Life Rhythms	41	Health & Wellness; Phys Ed
38	Thunderstorm	41	Science
39	Cold–Hot–Not	42	Any subject as source of words
40	Stuck!	43	Science
41	False Freeze	43	Any subject as source of True/False statements
42	Heads or Tails	45	Math
43	Ice Cube	45	Science; Language Arts
44	Number Shakes	45	Math

	Motivator	Page	Suggested Subject(s)
91	You DON'T Say!	73	Any
92	"Yes, But" Pet Peeves	73	Language Arts; Health & Wellness
93	Glad Game	74	Health & Wellness
94	Think Talk	74	Any
95	Fortunately / Unfortunately	75	Any
96	I Appreciate…	75	Health & Wellness; Social Studies
97	May There Be…	76	Any
98	Third-Person Talk	76	Language Arts
99	Hi-Lo Speak	77	Any
Let's Communicate: Brainstorm			
100	2-for-10 Tales	78	Language Arts
101	Point Please?	78	Social Studies; Language Arts
102	And the Real Meaning Is…	79	Language Arts
103	Synonym Sense	80	Language Arts
104	Go-Togethers	80	Any
105	Word Tennis	81	Language Arts; Any as source of theme
106	Quick Questions	81	Any
107	Big Word / Small Word	82	Language Arts
108	Excuses, Excuses	82	Any
109	Break-up	83	Language Arts

	Motivator	Page	Suggested Subject(s)
110	If They Could Talk…	83	Any
111	First and Last	84	Language Arts
Beyond the Three-Minute Mark			
112	Obstacle Course	85	Any
113	Let's Quiggle	86	Language Arts; Science; Math
114	Give Me a Clue	87	Science; Math; Language Arts; Health & Wellness
115	The Rule Rules!	88	Social Studies; Math; Language Arts
116	Back Talk	89	Social Studies; Math
117	Shake My Hand	89	Social Studies; Math; Science
118	Tell It Like It Is	90	Social Studies; Language Arts
119	Sense or Nonsense?	91	Language Arts; Any
120	It's MY Story!	91	Language Arts; Social Studies
121	The Expert	92	Social Studies; Science; Language Arts
122	And the Action Is…	93	Language Arts; Science; Social Studies
123	Action Telephone	93	Language Arts; Social Studies

3-Minute Motivators in Action

When introducing a 3-Minute Motivators to your class, it is good to reinforce these ideas:

- There is no wrong answer.
- Variety is good and is encouraged.
- All responses are celebrated.
- Private space, both physical and emotional, is always respected.

Once you have chosen a 3-Minute Motivator, take a few minutes first to browse the contents. Note that your spoken directions, the words you will say to the students, are presented in *italics*. Oral directions are presented in this manner to expedite presentation (all the teacher needs to do is read the brief notes to the class) and keep the motivators simple and quick to use. Naturally, the provided directions do not need to be used word-for-word; these are guidelines only. A quick read of the entire motivator will probably be sufficient for instant use.

Any non-italicized text within the activity steps (presented as a bulleted list) supplies additional directions. It may, for example, suggest that you "cue to start," or "remind students when they have 30 seconds remaining." Unlike the italicized cues, these are not meant to be read explicitly to the class.

Use the full list of steps on page 16 as a handy reference to using a 3-Minute Motivator. It includes the entire process, from Attention Cue to Concluding and Refocusing.

The Attention Cue

As every teacher knows, if the students aren't attending, teaching is a waste of time. So it is with 3-Minute Motivators. The students must be paying attention when the teacher introduces the activity. Thus, the activity is preceded by an attention cue that has been already established in the class. Some excellent cues include

- a short blast of a whistle
- use of any rhythm band instrument
- use of specific piece of music
- a clapping sequence led by you
- raising your hand and waiting silently until all students have hands raised
- rapping a squeaky hammer (or anything resembling a gavel) on your desk (This is my personal favorite as it simulates a courtroom, with the teacher as judge. My huge squeaky hammer works well with students at *any* level—even adult students!)

As with any situation in which a specific reaction is expected to a specific cue, the use of the cue must be first introduced, then cultivated and reinforced:

1. Introduce the cue and explain its purpose.
   When you hear this noise, you will immediately stop what you are doing and look at me.
2. Practice
   Everybody talk to a neighbor and be prepared to freeze when you hear this noise.
3. Reinforce
   - *Excellent! You all stopped talking and looked at me. That's exactly what I wanted you to do. This helps me because…*
   - *I'm so glad you all remembered to freeze on cue and look at me. Now I know you are ready to…*
   - *Thank you for freezing when you heard the cue. That's great! I know you want to …*

Repeat steps 2 and 3 frequently for the first few days, reinforcing consistently. Eventually, obeying the attention cue should become a classroom habit and can be reinforced intermittently.

The Importance of Concluding and Refocusing

Perhaps the most important aspect of successfully using a 3-Minute Motivator is the manner in which it is ended. A smooth transition is a necessary step that enables the teacher to bring the class back from an activity to the previously interrupted task or lesson. Although it takes only a few moments to make this crucial shift in focus, without it students may be left wondering what they just did, why they did it, and where they are supposed to be going as a result.

Once the motivator is finished to your satisfaction:

1. Cue for attention.
2. Quickly verbalize why the refocuser/motivator was carried out.
   I had the feeling none of you were really listening to the information about _____, so we (summarize the activity).
3. Concisely state current expectations for return to work.
   Now that you've had a chance to burn some energy (talk to a neighbor, move around a bit…), I need you to return to lesson and give it your full attention.
4. Provide positive reinforcement for return-to-work behaviors
5. Continue with the lesson or remind students what they were supposed to be doing pre-motivator.
   We were learning about_____ and I was explaining how to…

This entire "speech" should take no more than 30 seconds. Students will quickly learn that, although they have fun with the motivators, they are expected to return to work immediately following them.

> Concluding a 3-Minute Motivator follows a what–why–what pattern: *what* was done, *why* it was done, *what* is to be done now.

Class Participation

If some students are reluctant to cooperate and participate, even when the activity is presented as a game, allow them to choose to sit quietly at their desks and simply observe. It has been my experience that, after one or two times just observing, most students want to take part in activities, especially those that allow them imaginative freedom. On the other hand, many of the 3-Minute Motivators are entertaining to watch, so less-outgoing students may choose to enjoy them from this point of view; they still benefit from the refocusing quality of the motivator.

The main difficulty may be with students who wish to disrupt the class during the more quiet activities. The very nature of the Calm Down 3-Minute Motivators will be jeopardized if even a single student is noisy. Teachers must deal with these situations in whatever way works best for them, keeping in mind that the success of calming activities depends on room that is quiet for up to three minutes. If the student cannot or will not meet the three-minute criterion, it may be best to remove him or her for the short duration of the activity.

> Some motivators lend themselves to unusual competitive challenges; these can be enhanced with the addition of small prizes. It is not the size or quality of the prize that counts, but rather the idea of the prize that is, in itself, motivating. What's magical about the prizes associated with 3-Minute Motivators is that often they are won by students who seldom excel in other classroom pursuits.

Steps for Using a 3-Minute Motivator

1. Cue to gain attention

2. Briefly explain why the motivator is being used.

   I have lost you…
   You seem restless…
   I can see you need a break…
   You seem to need some talk time…

3. Explain the activity, using the directions included in each 3-Minute Motivator.

4. Remind students not to begin until you cue them to, and to stop or freeze again on cue.

5. Cue to begin.

6. Present the 3-Minute Motivator, using the script provided.

7. Cue to stop

8. Conclude and refocus by quickly summarizing what was done and why.

   We were all a bit restless so we just played _____. Now that you've used up a bit of energy, it's time to return to…

   You seemed sleepy and many of you were not paying attention, so we played _____. Now that you're all awake, let's get back to…

   I felt the need for a quick break, so we played _____. Now we can get back to…

- Make it fun, not punishment! Better to say, "Time for a refocuser. This is a little game…" than to say, "No one is on task and you are all talking, so we have to do something to change that…" The word *game* is the catch for kids.
- Always begin with your pre-established attention cue and end with a return to the interrupted or ensuing lesson.
- Always tell students *why* you chose to have them participate in a 3-Minute Motivator.
- Stick to the three-minute time frame as much as possible (unless you have a reason for varying the process). If you wish to debrief a motivator, keep it to about one minute, or say, "Remember what you just did/thought/saw /heard… and we'll talk about it after we finish our …(whatever you interrupted for the refocuser)."
- Use the term "refocuser" when referring to 3-Minute Motivators. The jargony term appeals to kids, and they start to look forward to the chance to "refocus."
- Remember the element of surprise. Keep your motivators fresh. Avoid using the same one over and over, and choose activities from different sections regularly. Mix them up.
- Note that directions for the teacher to say/read in *italics* mean that a motivator can be used instantaneously if necessary.
- It's a good idea to familiarize yourself with a few activities from each section, but don't feel you need to memorize the teacher's speaking directions.
- Don't feel forced to read class instructions exactly as they are written. These are guidelines only. You will certainly add your own flavor and make the motivators your own.
- Be sure the directions you provide (following the attention cue) are specific and exact. Remember that you want to reduce chaos, not create it.
- Use 3-Minute Motivators proactively rather than reactively. It is better to stop the lesson and interject a motivator when behaviors are just starting to wane, than when behaviors have escalated to the classroom bedlam all teachers face from time to time.
- Realize that Debrief, Extended Debrief, and Showcase prompts are suggestions only; you can choose to use them or ignore them.
- Realize that although a motivator may call for props, it will work well without them.
- Don't worry if a motivator bombs! Just admit defeat and return to the lesson. (Even a bombing activity serves, in its own way, to refocus.)
- Keep a record (perhaps using the 3-Minute Motivators at a Glance table on pages 11–13) of motivators that you have used effectively or ineffectively, which you would like to use again or would prefer to forget. Since the book contains so many motivators, this simple book-keeping will simplify future use of the activities.

At Your Desks

2

Calm Down

The motivators in this section require the least amount of physical activity as students remain seated silently at their desks throughout. With the teacher leading, students engage their imaginations in interesting, often unusual, ways. That these refocusing activities involve a degree of meditation, of quiet reflection and rumination, will quickly become obvious to teachers. What may be less obvious is how successfully students of all ages can handle, learn from, and appreciate such deliberations.

These motivators are most effective for situations where students have been very active; the teacher's goal is to calm them down in preparation for a more concentrated pursuit. For example, students may be off-task, talkative, out-of-desk, non-focused, or actively uninterested in the lesson or job at hand. There may be a general state of disorganization or hyperactivity in the room, or there may simply be too much contagious energy to allow for effective teaching and subsequent learning to take place.

These motivators may be useful on days when, for example, weather prohibits going outside for recess and students suffer from cabin fever, or when weekends or holidays are near and attentions are elsewhere. Or students may just have returned to class from a lively physical-education undertaking, an assembly, or other dynamic gathering that has invigorated them.

- To capitalize on the intention of relaxation the teacher should use a quiet, soothing, often monotone voice when providing the direction or presenting the scenarios. This is not a time for high passion and enthusiasm, but for a firm, tranquil, and composed intervention.
- Some of these calming motivators (Belly Breathing, Hug-a-Tree, Grounding Exercise, Zen Garden) work well before an important or intense seat-work activity, such as an exam. They may serve to reduce anxiety and encourage maximum effort.
- Most of the refocusers in this section take the form of "guided imagery," as the teacher calmly guides the thinking and internal visualization of the students. If some students reject this type of imagery, at least they will be sitting quietly with their eyes closed for the duration, and that in itself can serve as a positive experience.
- Most of these motivators work best on an individual basis; however, you may wish to debrief by encouraging quiet discussion between students as a natural follow-up.
- The opportunities for authentic discussion or follow-up writing are many, even if the particular refocuser does not include Debrief or Showcase notes. Neither of these literacy activities will lessen the effectiveness of the relaxing refocuser.

Calm Down

Subject: Health & Wellness

Individual

Note: Belly Breathing can be used *before* other motivators in this section, as an additional calming activity.

1. Belly Breathing

Objective: To breathe deeply and with control.

- *Sit quietly at your desk, hands folded.*
- *Close your eyes.*
- *Breathe normally.*
- *Now focus on your breathing: slowly **in** to a count of 5, hold for 5, slowly **out** for a count of 5.*
- *When you inhale, visualize yourself getting bigger and lighter. Air is rushing in to fill all your body cavities: chest, stomach, back, shoulders…*
- *When you hold your breath, visualize yourself getting lighter and lighter, even levitating.*
- *When you exhale, visualize yourself squeezing your lungs, getting rid of every bit of air, pushing it all out through your mouth. (This might make you cough, and that's okay. It just means you are getting all the dead air out.)*
- Teachers should remind students to keep their eyes closed, to continue breathing like this for about two minutes, and to silently count the seconds to themselves. Talk about "filling up like a balloon" when inhaling, and "squeezing your diaphragm down to your hips and sucking your tummy in" when exhaling.
- Allow students to continue for as long as they remain focused, or up to a maximum of two minutes, then say, *This will be your last breath. Slowly fill yourself up, count. Exhale and, as you curl down into yourself like a balloon losing all its air, you feel quiet, calm, relaxed…*

Calm Down

Subject: Science

Individual

Prop: Calming music from yoga, environmental sounds, relaxation CDs

2. Collecting Clouds

Objective: To attain a sense of calm by visualizing clouds.

- *Sit comfortably, feet on floor, heads on desks, arms comfortably wherever you want them*
- *Close your eyes and focus on your breathing. Allow about 15 seconds for this.*
- *Now, think of clouds—a beautiful clear blue sky and lots of clouds.*
- *What do your clouds look like? See them in your mind. Really look at them.*
  - *What shapes are they? Are they changing shape?*
  - *Are they moving?*
- *Imagine you are floating on one of the clouds*
  - *What does it feel like?*
  - *What can you see?*
- Allow this to continue silently for up to 30 seconds or until you note restlessness, then continue: *Now come back down to earth, but keep feeling the gentle movement of the clouds as you sit up quietly.*

Extended Debrief: Pre-writing, illustrating, etc.

Showcase: Sharing of extended debrief products.

Calm Down

Subjects: Art; Health & Wellness
Individual

Prop: Calming music from yoga, environmental sounds, relaxation CDs, even classical music

3. Hearing Colors

Objective: To attach imaginary colors to sounds.

- *Sit quietly at your desk, feet on the floor, heads on desktops. Close your eyes.*
- *You are going to hear some music. Listen to it and see in your mind the colors the music makes you think of.*
- Play the music. Wait for 10 seconds then say, *What colors do you see?*
  - *Think color. Does the music make you think of green? Or maybe pink?*
  - *Concentrate on the colors of the rainbow and try to visualize which shades this music makes you think of.*
  - *Breathe deeply and think color.*
- *I am going to stop the music. When I do, you will sit up quietly and think of the color or colors you saw in your mind.*

Debrief: Students can quietly share visualized colors; or you can conduct a quick survey of the predominant colors.

Calm Down

Subjects: Language Arts; Art
Individual

4. Magic Carpet

Objective: To experience sensory awareness.

- *Sit quietly, feet on floor, head on hands on desk.*
- *Close your eyes and breathe deeply.*
- *I am going to take you away from here on a magic-carpet ride.*
- *Imagine you are not sitting in your desk; you are on a beautiful carpet. Think these things in your mind:*
  - *What does your carpet look like? What color is it? What does it feel like?*
- *Now the carpet is going to start moving. It is slowly rising up, slowly… rising… getting higher.*
  - *What does it feel like now?*
  - *Can you feel the gentle movement?*
  - *Pay attention to the gentle breeze in your face as your special carpet moves higher and higher.*
- *You feel very comfortable. You are high above the clouds. You are totally relaxed as your carpet sails along like a bird in the air.*
- *Now imagine where you are going. This is your carpet so you can make it go wherever you want it to.*
  - *Where would you like your carpet to take you?*
  - *You can look down if you want to, in your mind. What do you see? Where are you going?*
- *Now I'm going to stop talking and I want you to remain on your carpets for 60 seconds, just flying wherever you want to, feeling happy and peaceful.*
- After 60 seconds bring them back by saying, *Now you are going to come back to earth. Let your carpet come down gently, slowly, until you are back in your desk.*

Debrief: *Discuss details of your trip with another student.*

Extended Debrief: Class discussion leading to literacy assignment

Showcase: The creation of visuals, stories, descriptions for sharing.

Calm Down

Subject: Depends on topic
Individual

5. Imagine This

Objective: To experience the sights, smells, and sounds of an imaginary outing.

- *Sit quietly at your desk, feet on floor, heads on desks.*
- *Close your eyes and breathe deeply.*
- *I am going to take you to an imaginary place. I want you to concentrate on everything you see, hear, smell and feel. First just concentrate on your breathing –in–out–in–out…*
- *You are lost in the wilderness. (See list in box for additional Situations.) It is a lovely day, but you are lost.*
- *Look around in your mind. What do you see? What do you hear? What time of day is it? How do you feel?*
- *Walk around slowly. Look at everything.*
  - *Pay attention to the sounds.*
  - *Pay attention to the smells*
- Continue in this manner, focusing on different aspects of sensory awareness depending on the "location" or theme chosen. The idea is to force students to "be" in this setting and really focus on it in their minds.
- As this motivator is intended to be soothing, keep the images positive. Avoid taking the students' thoughts to negative situations.

Debrief: I strongly encourage debriefing this activity. This can be quick (assuming you want to return to your previous lesson). Simply have students share where they were and what any dominant images were.

Extended Debrief: Since students can experience very strong images, they like to share these either with peers or on paper. The images might make ideas for future writing: at this point they can be quickly jotted down in students' writing-idea books; a whole-class discussion could take place prior to a literacy task.

* * *

Suggested Situations

- In space
- At an old-fashioned farm
- At an amusement park
- On top of a ski hill
- In a plane over the mountains
- At the ocean
- In the Arctic
- Under the sea
- In a magic kingdom
- On the moon
- Inside a huge tree
- In a meadow filled with flowers

Calm Down

Subject: Science

Individual

6. Time Machine

Objective: To imagine travelling forward or backward in time.

- *Sit quietly at your desks, feet on the floor, heads resting comfortably on your desks.*
- *Breathe deeply; focus on your breathing. Relax completely.*
- *You are very lucky today. You are going to go inside a time machine. Just keep listening to my voice to find out how to do this.*
- *First imagine where you'd like to go.*
  - *Into the past? To the ages of dinosaurs or cave men?*
  - *Or into the future? On a rocket ship? On an alien planet?*
- *Take a few breaths to decide silently where you will travel.*
- Wait for about 15 seconds. Then say, *I will count back from ten and, when I get to one, your time machine will whisk you off to your chosen time and place. Get ready—10, 9, 8, 7, 6, 5, 4, 3, 2, 1. Go!*
- Wait for a few seconds then say, *You are there.*
  - *Breathe deeply and take time to look around. What do you see? What do you hear? Smell? Feel?*
- *For the next 60 seconds really pay attention to this magical time and place. Nothing bad can happen here because you chose a perfect place. Just enjoy it.*
- Wait for about 60 seconds, then say, *When I count up from one to ten, your time machine will start to bring you home again. Here we go—1, 2, 3, 4, 5, 6, 7, 8, 9, 10!*
  - *Keep your eyes closed for a few seconds and remember everything you saw and felt.*
- *Now slowly sit up and open your eyes.*

Debrief: I strongly encourage debriefing this activity. This can be quick (assuming you want to return to your previous lesson). Simply have students share with a partner where they were and what any dominant images were.

Extended Debrief: Since students can experience very strong images, they like to share these either with peers or on paper. The images might make ideas for future writing, drama activities, or art projects: ideas could be quickly jotted down in students' writing-idea books; a whole-class discussion could take place prior to a summative task.

Calm Down

Subjects: Any; Health & Wellness

Individual

7. Chocolate & Bricks

Objective: To release frustrations and appreciate something good.

- *Sit comfortably, feet on the floor, hands together, eyes closed.*
- *Relax and breathe deeply*
- *I want you to start to think of something or someone that really annoys you or makes you angry. Now concentrate on the bad feeling—the anger and frustration. Feel it: you are all tense and angry. Feel it in your stomach, in your head—everywhere. I am going to give you 10 seconds to really experience that bad feeling.*
- Wait 10 seconds. *Now take that nasty feeling and cement it inside a solid brick.*
  - *Push it into a brick.*
  - *Close the opening with cement*
  - *Now you have a heavy, hard brick with the bad feeling inside*
- *Now comes the fun part. In your mind you get to blow up that brick—WAIT until I give you the Blast cue. When I say "Blast," you will imagine blowing up the brick into millions of tiny pieces, The bad feeling will be completely gone.*
- *Get ready—look closely at the brick with your annoying thing inside it. BLAST!*
- *Keep your eyes closed.*
- *Now think of something or someone that makes you very happy. See that thing or person; feel the good feeling; really try to experience the good feeling you get from the thing or person. You feel warm and comfy inside. You are smiling to yourself. I'll give you a few seconds to really feel the good feeling.*
- Wait for about 10 seconds. *Now take the feeling that the good thing gives you and cover it in chocolate. Look at the good feeling all covered in chocolate.*
  - *What sort of a shape does it make?*
  - *Can you smell that delicious chocolate?*
- *Now, when I tell you to, in your mind you are going to eat the chocolate. When you do that, the good feeling will stay inside you, making you all warm and tingly.*
- *Ready? Look at the chocolate-covered good feeling. Eat it.*

Extended Debrief: This is an excellent activity to follow with individual journal reflections. Guiding questions might be

- How did it feel when you blew up the brick?
- How did it feel when you ate the chocolate?
- Were the feelings different? The same?

Calm Down

Subject: Any
Individual

Notes: This is perfect for pre-exam situations.

- Attempt to speak in a slow, quiet monotone for this exercise.

8. Grounding Exercise

Objective: To experience a total sense of calm by using a grounding or centring-of-self technique borrowed from Eastern philosophies.

- *Sit comfortably, feet flat on floor. Don't slouch; sit up straight.*
- *Put your hands together on your desk.*
- *Move slightly away from the back of your seat so that you are not leaning against it.*
- *Relax your tongue. Let it lie gently in your mouth. Relax your jaw.*
- *Close your eyes and breathe deeply and quietly—in through your nose, out through your mouth. In–out. In–out…*
- Wait for 10 seconds before continuing. *Now imagine you see a beautiful golden ball floating before you. Look at it—it's swirling and shining and sparkling. So beautiful.*
- *Watch it. Really look at in your mind. Keep thinking, "Beautiful golden ball…"*
- Repeat these phrases as many times as needed to allow students to calm down. You will need to use your judgment here, remembering that not all students will have the same experience.
- *Now look closely. The beautiful golden ball is moving toward you—closer, closer.*
- *It is moving* **inside** *you, right into your stomach.*
- *The beautiful golden ball is* **in** *your stomach (or* tummy*). It is making you feel warm, relaxed, wonderful…*
- *Feel the ball filling you with golden light, making you calm, confident, relaxed and happy…*
- *Keep enjoying the feel of the golden ball in your stomach until you hear the Stop cue.*
- Wait for up to 60 seconds then say, *Stop. Let the ball go and open your eyes.*

Debrief: A quick sharing of "how it felt" is useful here, especially if it's the first time this technique has been used.

Extended Debrief: Excellent to extend to journal reflections. For many students, this technique may be quite surprising and refreshing.

Calm Down

Subjects: Science; Health & Wellness
Individual

9. Hug-a-Tree

Objective: To experience the sensory imagery of hugging a tree.

- *Sit comfortably at your desk, feet on floor.*
- *Close your eyes and stretch across your desktop.*
- *Spread your arms wide, resting them on the desktop.*
- *Slowly bring your arms together as if hugging a tree.*
- *Stop moving your arms when you get to the size of your tree trunk.*
- *Keep hugging the tree and in your mind, visualize what your special tree looks like, feels like, smells like.*
- *Keep hugging gently and feel the calm strength of the tree entering you, relaxing you, making you feel relaxed and peaceful.*

Calm Down

Subjects: Health & Wellness; Social Studies

Individual

10. Silent Scream

Objective: To demonstrate strong emotion(s) using body language only.

- *We all have many strong feelings—emotions. Sometimes we are not able to show these because of where we are or who we are with. We are going to practice some silent emotions.*
- *Sit tall, facing the front, eyes on me. These expressions of emotions are for you only; it's not necessary to watch other students.*
- *Begin by thinking of being very sad. Think unhappiness and feel it with your body—your eyes, your head, your chest, your hands. Breathe slowly. Very very sad—feel it and let your body show it for 10 seconds.*
- Take the students through each of these emotions: anger, fear, worry, pride, hunger, excitement.
- End with a positive emotion such as happiness, peacefulness, joy, relaxation, or contentment.

Debrief: A quick review of how it felt to show emotion without words.

Extended Debrief: Journalling about an emotion difficult or easy to express silently.

Showcase: Choose who you want to showcase based on what you know about individual students.

Calm Down

Subject: Any

Individual

11. Absolutely Nothing!

Objective: To do absolutely nothing for as long as possible.

- *This is a tough game. You are going to do NOTHING!*
- *Start by sitting comfortably in your chair. You can put your heads on your desks if you want to. Just be sure you are very comfortable.*
- *When I give the Start cue, you are going to freeze—not move at all, not make a single sound—for a full minute. Sounds easy doesn't it? It's not.*
- *So check to see if you are comfy and in a position you can hold without moving—not even to scratch!*
- You can work up to 60 seconds (and more). It's difficult for students to remain motionless and silent for this amount of time.

Debrief: Discuss what was difficult/easy about the game.

Extended Debrief: Challenge students to think of situations where total immobility and silence might be necessary.

| **Calm Down**
Subject: Language Arts
Individual | **12. The Key**

Objective: To creatively imagine what could be done with a mysterious key. |

- *Sit comfortably. You can put your heads on your desks if you want to.*
- *Close your eyes and breathe deeply. Listen to my voice.*
- *I want you to visualize—see in your mind—a huge, shiny key. The key is as large as your fist. Look at it.*
  - *What shape is it?*
  - *What color?*
- *Think only about that amazing key. It will open whatever door you want.*
- *Start thinking of everything you will see when the key opens doors.*
- Wait for about 20 seconds before continuing: *Now choose just one of those doors to open. Use your magic key to open it and take yourself on a magical journey.*
- Wait about 20 seconds. *Take time to see, hear, smell, and maybe even taste everything behind your magical door. Pay attention to color, texture, odor. Stay in your magical place until I give you the Stop cue.*

Extended Debrief: This is an excellent pre-writing activity, as long as some discussion occurs between the guided imagery and the writing process.

| **Calm Down**
Subject: Science
Individual | **13. Lift Off!**

Objective: To imagine the body levitating or lifting out of the desk into the air. |

- *Sit comfortably in your desk, feet flat on the floor. Rest your head on your arms and close your eyes.*
- *Breathe deeply in through your nose, out through your mouth.*
- *Be silent and listen to my voice.*
- *You feel very heavy, like a solid rock. Heavy, heavy… Think of pressure pushing down on you—pushing hard, making you heavier and heavier.*
- *Keep thinking of the pressure and the heaviness of your body—your legs, your arms, your head…*
- Wait for about 20 seconds before continuing: *Now something magical is happening. Suddenly you feel the pressure being lifted off.*
- *Your feet and legs start to feel light. They almost lift right off the floor.*
- *Your body feels lighter and lighter.*
- *The light feeling moves into your shoulders, head, arms…Lighter, lighter…*
- *You are so light you start to feel yourself lift right off the chair in your mind—not in reality, remember. Lighter, lighter,…*
- *Now imagine you are actually lifting up, rising up into the air—slowly, like a weightless bubble. Lifting, rising… Rising up, up, up…Lighter and lighter…*
- Continue coaching them in this way for as long as you feel is appropriate, then cue them with, *You will gently float around until you hear the Stop cue.*

Debrief: *What did it feel like?* Encourage sharing between students for a few seconds before returning to the interrupted lesson.

Calm Down

Subjects: Art; Health & Wellness

Individual

Props: Pencils and unlined paper

14. Zen Garden

Objective: To trace curved lines with fingers for up to 60 seconds.

- *Take out a clean piece of paper, one without lines, and a pencil or pen.*
- *When I give the Start cue, you will fill the paper with gently waving lines, going from the top of the page to the bottom.*
- *You will begin by drawing a single line like this.* Model a curvy line on the board. Avoid making it complicated; it should be a gentle curve such as might be seen in a Zen garden.
- *Now you will fill the page by drawing other lines close to, but not touching, the first line.*
- *Leave a space of 1/4 inch/2–3 cm between the lines.*
- *Every line will follow the first line until your page is filled.*
- *When you are finished, put your pen down and sit quietly waiting for the next instruction.*
- Allow about 30 seconds for this, or until students are finished. Side coach as necessary.
- *Now when I give the Start cue, use your fingers to slowly follow the curved lines from top to bottom, over and over again.*
- *Follow the lines and focus on the gentle curves.*
- *Touch softly, gently; your fingers barely touch the paper.*
- *You will keep doing this until I give the Stop cue.*

Debrief: Quickly discuss how it felt to carry out this task. Most students find it extremely calming.

Calm Down

Subject: Science

Individual

15. Telescope

Objective: To imagine looking at an object through a very powerful telescope.

- *Sit comfortably with your feet on the floor and your heads on your arms.*
- *Close your eyes.*
- *If you prefer to sit up straight and close your eyes, that's okay too.*
- *You are very comfortable.*
- *Breathe deeply in through your nose, out through your mouth.*
- *Now I want you imagine you have in front of you a very powerful telescope. This telescope will allow you to see in great detail anything you want to see.*
  - *For example you might want to look at your own hand and see all the tiny lines, colors, wrinkles…whatever.*
  - *Or you might want to look at something far away, like the moon. You could see all the details of the surface of the moon.*
- *I want you to think for a few seconds about what it is you'll examine through your telescope. Don't look through it yet. Just think of what you will examine. I'll tell you when to look through the telescope.*
- Wait for about 20 seconds, then cue students to begin looking. Side coach for a few seconds, then remain quiet for up to two minutes.

Debrief: Invite students to share what they were examining. This should be a very quick "once around the room" sharing.

Extended Debrief: Write or discuss the detailed images.

Pencil and Paper

Useful at any time when students simply need a break, Pencil and Paper activities are especially useful following a more physical class, such as a movement, Phys Ed, or Fine Arts class. In these instances, they serve as a transition from a big activity full of movement to a smaller or more focused seatwork activity.

The motivators in this section continue to keep students at their desks, but differ from Calm Down activities in that they involve more active, often more stimulating, involvement. Because students will be required to think and react quickly using paper and pencils, these tasks tend to be more cognitive and arousing. Many of them are competitive in nature, encouraging fast reactions (Scrabble Scramble, page 35), careful predictions (Never-ending Line, page 31), or directed thinking (Written Rumor, page 33). Students love these motivators mainly because creativity is encouraged in a context where no response is incorrect. They work well before lessons requiring careful penmanship (Zoom-out, page 34), fine motor control (Mirror Images, page 37), active listening, such as to a teacher presentation (Draw My Words, page 31), or literacy concepts (Letter Scramble, page 30).

Unlike the Calm Down activities for individual students, these motivators all involve working with partners or small groups:

Teachers will all have their own favorite ways to pair students, but a little advance thought as to which method will be used will prevent possible arguments and classroom disruption.

- Often the quickest way to have children pair off is to simply have them partner with an adjacent student: *Turn to the person behind/beside you.*
- Another quick way is to have students number-off: 1 and 2 are partners, as are 3 and 4, and so on.
- It is always a good idea to change the system regularly to encourage new relationships and provide the opportunity for all students to work with, and learn from, each other.

Pencil and Paper

Subject: Any

Partners

Note: This is a silent activity.

16. Box Me In

Objective: To avoid being boxed-in in a simple game of chance and cognition.

- *Sit as close together as possible. You may have to move a chair and use one desk between you for this game.*
- *You each need a pencil; you need one piece of paper between you.*
- *Put four dots across the page about an inch/2.5 cm apart, then put four dots going down, then fill in the square. You will have 16 dots altogether.* Model on board: a 4-by-4 square made up of dots.
- *Here's the game. Decide who will start.* Wait until they decide.
- *Starter connects any two dots to make a straight line. Then the other person connects any two dots, and so on.*
- *Here's the trick. The boxes represent little jails. You want to stay out of them. That means you do NOT want to be forced to draw the last line that completes a box. If you do, you must put your initial IN that box—go to jail—and take another turn.*
- *The person with the LEAST number of initials in boxes is the winner, because he/she has been to jail the least number of times.*
- *Remember that this is a silent activity.*

Pencil and Paper

Subjects: Science; Math

Partners

Note: No oral communication allowed.

17. Circles & Squares

Objective: To create, with a partner, an interesting illustration or abstract picture using only circles and squares, using no oral communication.

- *Decide between you who will be the circle and who will be the square.*
- *You and your partner will have two minutes to create an interesting picture.*
- *But here's the catch—you can use only your designated shape. The squares can draw only squares and the circles can draw only circles.*
- *AND…you can't talk to each other. You just have to start drawing—taking turns—and see what happens.*
- Cue to start.
- Warn students when there are only 30 seconds left.
- Cue to stop.
- *You now have 30 seconds to discuss with your partner what your drawing could be. Maybe it's an abstract. Maybe it looks like something. Decide now. Stop after 30 seconds.*

Debrief: Quickly allow each pair to show and name their drawing.

Pencil and Paper

Subject: Any

Partners

18. O's and X's

Objective: To play a paper and pencil game, the opposite to the familiar "X's and O's."

- *This game is like the game you know as "X's and O's" but it's just the opposite.*
- *Start by drawing two vertical lines and two horizontal lines through them. Model the grid.*
- *You now have nine empty boxes.*
- *Decide who is X and who is O.*
- *Take turns putting your signs in boxes. Your job is to avoid making a straight line with your sign.*
- *If your partner forces you to make a straight line, you're out.*

Pencil and Paper

Subject: Language Arts

Partners

19. Letter Scramble

Objective: To randomly write five letters, then add these to a partner's five letters to make words.

- *Begin with each partner putting five letters on your page. But don't let your partner see what you're writing.*
- *Now, put together the letters you have both written, and make as many words from these letters as possible.*
- *If you both have chosen the same letter, that means you can use that letter twice in a word. Otherwise each letter can only be used once in a word.*
- *You will have two minutes. Go!*
- At the end of two minutes, check for winning pairs. Do a quick check for accuracy. Point out that a lot is dependent upon which letters they initially chose. Once students have played this game a few times, they become expert at selecting the letters that naturally morph into the maximum number of words.

Pencil and Paper

Subject: Any as source of words

Partners

Prop: A list of 10–15 (or 20–25) words.

Note: A grid of two vertical and two horizontal lines means students can choose nine words, increasing the difficulty level. In this case, teachers should have 20–25 words from which to select.

20. 4-Word Lotto

Objective: To randomly select words with a partner, and take a chance that they will be the words chosen by the teacher.

- *Make a large + on your page, made of two lines intersecting.*
- *From our list of words, choose any four and write one in each square.*
- Words can be core-subject related, word-wall related, spelling related, or just randomly chosen. Teachers can have them already written on slips of paper, or students can choose them as a group.
- *I will randomly draw a word from the list. If you have that word, draw a line through it.*
- *The first couple to have lines through all their words wins.*
- Selecting lotto words from subject areas helps with vocabulary reinforcement and spelling. Teachers can choose to provide the definitions of the words, rather than the words themselves, if they wish to reinforce meaning.

Pencil and Paper

Subjects: Art; Math or Science

Partners

Note: No oral communication allowed.

21. Never-ending Line

Objective: To draw a picture with a partner, sharing a single pencil and using a non-stopping line.

- *Each pair of you should have one sheet of unlined paper and one pencil.*
- *You and your partner are to create an interesting picture—but there's a catch. Once you put the pencil on the paper, you cannot lift the pencil again until I give the Stop cue.*
- *Your picture will be made from one continuous, never-ending line, and you'll take turns making it.*
- *Every time you hear my cue, exchange the pencil. The person receiving the pencil picks up where the partner stopped and keeps going.*
- *But there's another catch. You can't discuss what you are making. It just has to grow out of the line you are making.* Model or give an example using students' names.
- Cue to start. Cue every five seconds or so, for up to about two minutes.
- *Now you and your partner have 20 seconds to decide what your picture is. Then we'll quickly share.*

Debrief: Invite each pair to hold up their drawing and tell what it is.

Pencil and Paper

Subjects: Art; Science; Language Arts

Partners

22. Draw My Words

Objective: To "copy" an illustration by listening to a partner's directions.

- *Decide who will be the Speaker and who will be the Artist.*
- *All Artists must now turn away from the front of the room.* (Assuming use of overhead, you don't want them to see the illustration or word depicting an illustration.)
- Make the illustration (best with younger students) or word clearly visible to the Speakers. Picture props (overhead illustrations of simple objects) can be used or students can draw these themselves from spoken directions.

- *Now, Speakers, your job is to get your partner to reproduce/draw this illustration/word by giving them cues.*
- *BUT you can't tell them what they are drawing. The only directions you can provide are words for shape, lines, or placement on the page.*
  - *For example, you might say, "At the top of the page draw a circle."*
- *You have two minutes to talk your partner through the entire drawing.*
- *Cue to start and stop.*

Showcase: Invite sharing of diagrams.

*   *   *

Possible illustrations

- Fish, mermaids, octopuses, whales, jellyfish, starfish
- Animals such as rabbits, cats, dogs, elephants, giraffes, turtles
- Cars, trucks, trains, boats
- Stick people "in action"
- Flowers, trees, birds, butterflies, lady bugs
- House, barn, church, teepee, tent, hut

Pencil and Paper

Subject: Math

Partners

23. Number Madness

Objective: To use previously chosen numbers to arrive at teacher-provided numerals.

- Pair students and be sure each pair has two pieces of paper and two pencils.
- *Divide your page into four by making a big + in the middle.*
- *In each quadrant, put a number between 0 and 9.*
- *The other page is for keeping score.*
- *Now, I will say a number. If you have that number written on your page, give yourself a point on the score page.*
- *However, if you can* **make** *that number, by adding/subtracting/dividing/ multiplying* (teacher decides which operation to use depending on student abilities), *then give yourself a point. You and your partner can quickly discuss this possibility.*
  - *For example, if I have both the numbers 1 and 3 on my page, and the number called is 4, then I can add 1 and 3 to get 4. I get a point.*
- *But here's the catch. If I use two or more numbers to get the called number, I write the operation in the quadrant of the first number used in that operation.*

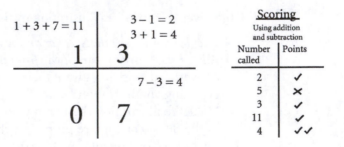

Pencil and Paper

Subject: Language Arts
Small Group (5–6)

24. Written Rumor

Objective: To write and rewrite a statement, and observe the changes.

- *For this game you will need a pen or pencil each, and one sheet of paper per group.*
- *Each person will read a sentence written by the person before him or her, then will hide that sentence from view by folding the paper.* Model how to fold paper horizontally to cover the sentence.
- *Then you will rewrite the sentence so that it means the same thing—or almost the same thing—but you will try to use different words.*
  - *For example, if the sentence says, "I went to town to buy groceries," I could write, "I went to the store to buy bread and milk."*
- *Each person will just have a few seconds to silently read, rewrite, and pass it on.*
- *This is a timed game. At the end of 60 seconds, we will share what each group has written as a final remark.*

Debrief: Share the final writings. Quickly discuss how they have changed and why.

Extended Debrief: This activity lends itself to in-depth discussions of how and why rumors start, gather speed, get corrupted, etc.

* * *

Possible Opening Sentences

- The animals in the jungle were in danger of extinction.
- The students ran from the school when the fire alarm went off.
- In my kitchen there are cooking utensils and food.
- My backpack is a thing of wonder because it hold so many precious items.
- The movie was scary but the popcorn was buttery and good.
- All the kids in our class have good work skills, good manners, and good hairstyles.
- I have a perfect pet because it is small and cuddly.

Pencil and Paper

Subject: Language Arts
Partners

Note: No oral communication allowed.

25. Shared-Pen Stories

Objective: To write a sentence or short story by "sharing" a single writing tool.

- Pair students and provide a single piece of blank paper per pair; consider pairing heterogeneously (not always "the person next to you").
- *You are going to write a (story, sentence)together, but you cannot talk about what you are going to write.*
- *I will give you a topic, then partner A will start writing whatever comes to mind.*
- *When I (provide the stop cue; e.g., clap, whistle) partner B will take the pen and continue on from where A left off.*
- *Remember—no talking. You just have to guess what your partner might have been going to say.*

- *When a thought is finished, put a period after it and continue writing until the cue.*
- Provide the cue approximately every ten seconds. (This may need to be adjusted according to students' age.)
- *When I tell you to stop, you will read over what you have written together and be prepared to share.*

Debrief: *Share your sentence/story with another pair (or whole class). How good were you at figuring out what your partner was thinking?*

*   *   *

Write About

- Pet peeves
- Homework
- Sisters or brothers
- Friends

Pencil and Paper

Subject: Science

Partners

Note: An excellent resource for this type of thinking is the picture book *Zoom* by Istvan Banyai.

26. Zoom-Out

Objective: To create a picture/illustration that begins with a very tiny detail and works outward.

- Pair students and provide a single piece of blank paper per pair.
- *Your job will be to create something that quite naturally starts small and gets larger.*
  - *For example, this is sort of like looking first at your fingernail, then gradually at your whole body.*
- *For this activity there can be quiet talking as you and your partner figure out what you are drawing. It might take a few moments for you to do this.*
- *In the meantime, you must keep adding to the picture. Maybe nothing will grow out of your picture and it will end up being an abstract or design, and that's okay too.*
- *Partner A, please draw a dot in the centre of the page.*
- *Now Partner B, without discussion, add something to the dot. Keep it small.*
- *Now each time I signal (use the cue), you will hand over the pencil and keep taking turns adding something to the drawing, moving from the centre of the page outward.*
- Cue every ten seconds or so. If students are stuck, make suggestions such as *Maybe it could be an eye, a spot on something, a button, a pimple.* Once students get the idea, this task truly catapults.

Debrief: *Were you able to create an actual representation of something? Name your illustration*

Extended Debrief: *Where in science do we look closely at things like this? Discuss/write about this concept.*

Showcase: *Share your illustration with another partnership (or the whole class.).*

Subjects: Language Arts; Any as source of theme

Partners

27. Scrabble Scramble

Objective: To create a crossword puzzle using words related to a theme.

- Give each pair of students a sheet of paper with a grid, such as graph paper; the size of the squares should be sized according to the age/ability of your students.
- *This activity involves you being creative with words and putting them together to form a crossword puzzle—just like playing Scrabble.*
- *I will give you the words. You and your partner are to pick any one you want to begin with, then try to fit in as many of the others as you can.*
- *You will have two minutes* (or more, depending on your purpose) *to see who can fit the most words together.*

Debrief: Survey to see how many words were correctly used. Select winners.

Extended Debrief: Make further use of the created puzzles by having students write definitions in appropriate crossword style. They can then exchange with other pairs to complete the blank crosswords.

Pencil and Paper

Subject: Any

Partners

Note: No oral communication allowed.

28. Add-Ons

Objective: To create a drawing taking turns adding components.

- Pair students and provide each pair with paper and a pencil. Have them decide which partner will be A, and which will be B.
- *This game involves careful cooperation with your partner. You will take turns drawing, but each of you only draw a single part of the illustration.*
  - *For example, if you were drawing a house, partner A might draw the roof, then partner B might add the sides, and so on.*
- *The trick is that you can't talk to each other; you'll have to figure out what your partner is trying to draw by watching and imagining.*
- *I will tell you what to begin with. A will draw that, then B will draw, and so on.*
- *At the beginning, keep your drawings fairly small so that you can keep adding on to them without running out of space.*
- *Remember—only one part of the drawing per person.*
- Watch that students don't "keep the pencil" to draw more than a single component at a time. Use the cue approximately every ten seconds to indicate when to change partners.

Debrief: *Stop drawing and discuss with your partner how well your combined drawing went—or didn't go.*

Extended Debrief: You may want to post or share some or all of the results, or follow-up with personal reflections in journals.

* * *

Possible Starts

• a circle "face"	• a tree	• a hat
• a bird	• a roof with a chimney	• a wheel
• a stick man	• a wagon	• a hand

Pencil and Paper

Subjects: Health & Wellness; Language Arts; Social Studies (theme of haves and have-nots)

Individual

Props: Blindfolds, or students can be instructed to close their eyes and not peek

29. Blind Draw

Objective: To try to draw (or write) without looking.

- *For this game you will work alone.*
- *In fact, you will be more alone than usual as you will be blindfolded (or keeping your eyes closed).*
- *You job will be to write (or draw) without looking at your page.*
- *You will begin and stop on cue.*
- *Start by feeling the edges of your page before you put on your blindfold (or close your eyes).*
- *I will tell you what to write (or draw).*
- *Ready? Begin. Keep writing (or drawing) until I cue to stop.*

Debrief: *Uncover your eyes and look at your work. How good is it? You may share it with a neighbor. Why was that difficult?*

Extended Debrief: You may wish to tie this activity to lessons about differentiation, handicaps, or even the concept of having less than others in our society or in the world in general.

Pencil and Paper

Subject: Any

Partners

30. Snowglobe Drawings

Objective: To connect random dots into a reasonable facsimile of a picture.

- *Pair up and decide who's A and who's B.*
- *Partner B, you will think of a snowglobe, pretend you are inside one, and draw the snowflakes all over your page. In other words, fill the page with dots.*
- *However, I am going to put a limit on the number of snowflakes in your globe; you have only _____.* Choose a number from 20 to 40; use fewer dots for younger students as the more dots there are, the more difficult the task.
- *OK, begin. B, make dots anywhere you want on the page.*
- *Now it's A's turn. A, you must find a way to connect these dots to make a picture. And you have to use them all. Maybe your picture will have to be an abstract.*
- *You have one minute to do this.*
- Have the students switch roles so both have a chance to try each part of this creative activity. Students are much more adept at joining random dots than adults are, and you may be surprised at the results.

Debrief: *You may have a few moments to talk about your pictures with other students.*

Extended Debrief: Invite students to share with the class if they wish to.

Pencil and Paper

Subjects: Language Arts; Science; Math

Partners

31. Mirror Images

Objective: To create symmetrical illustrations or designs.

- *Everyone has looked in mirrors. When you do this, the image you see is actually the opposite of yourself.*
- *Now one of you will be the mirror.*
- *Begin by folding your paper lengthwise to make a crease, then opening it flat again.*
- *Decide who's A and who's B.*
- *A, you will work on the right side of the crease; B will work on the left.*
- *A, you begin by drawing some simple thing: an object such as an apple or a flower.* (It may be easier for some students to start with single lines—a curved line, a diagonal line—before moving to shapes).
- *B, you try to reproduce a symmetrical mirror-image, the way it would look in a mirror.*
- *Now B, you add something to the image, and A will copy it.*
- *You will continue in this manner until I cue you to stop.*
- An alternate, more difficult, way to handle this task is to have the student who is using the left side of the paper use his or her left hand to draw.

Debrief: *Look closely at your pages. Is one side exactly symmetrical to the other? How can you check?* (Refold on the crease and hold up to the light to see if the lines correspond.)

Extended Debrief: You may wish to discuss problems with this task, or where, in nature or real life, symmetry exists.

3

Up and At 'Em

These activities are visible to all and, therefore, are more entertaining than those in the previous chapter. The magic of these refocusers lies in the beautiful hyperactivity-reduction fostered by the restricted, seated actions.

Get Moving

The 3-Minute Motivators in this section are designed to provide students with a controlled escape for energy while at the same time energizing those who may be bored or sleepy. In most cases children remain seated at their own desks, but are involved in innovative, teacher-led, movement-based activities—on their own. They will be involved in a variety of low-risk activities that will challenge them to be creative and focused. Cognition, imagination, short-term memory, and fine motor skills all come into play, as well as accurate looking, listening to directions, and deciphering nonverbal communication cues.

- Most of these 3-Minute Motivators are individual pursuits; students perform them on their own. In some instances, however, the individuals become a part of the whole-class activity (e.g., Thunderstorm, page 41).
- Most Get Moving motivators are silent activities, and teachers will need to reinforce this aspect. Communication may still be ongoing, but it is nonverbal communication. Before beginning the movement, reinforce that this is a silent activity.
- Teachers will probably choose Get Moving refocusers if they want to engage students actively, yet minimize student interactions. However, whole-class discussions can easily follow any of the activities.

Get Moving

Subject: Any, especially where fine motor control is required

Individual; Partners

Note: This is a good hand exercise; using it prior to a lengthy writing exercise may be useful.

32. Open–Shut–Shake

Objective: To mimic increasingly difficult hand movements.

- *Sit straight in your desk, feet on the floor, eyes on me.*
- *I am going to model a hand movement that will be either opening/closing hands(O/C), or a shake of the hands.* Demonstrate by opening/closing hands once and shaking loose hands twice.
- *Your job is to repeat exactly what I have done.*
- Begin simply: e.g., three shakes, three O/C. Then increase difficulty: e.g., one O/C, two shakes, four O/C, one shake, etc. The increasing difficulty keeps students on their toes.
- Invite students to take turns being the leader.
- Or invite students to turn to a partner and create an innovative combination or O/C plus shakes—one they can share with the whole class.

Showcase: Invite students to prepare a demonstration piece.

---

33. Puppet Master

Objective: To experience being controlled by marionette strings.

- *Sit quietly at your desk, feet on floor, arms draped across desk, head on desk.*
- *Close your eyes.*
- *You are going to become a marionette, a puppet on strings.*
- *I am the puppeteer. When I tell you I am pulling a certain string, you move only that part of your body.*
- *Relax completely. You are a puppet with no bones. Breathe deeply.*
- *Now I am gently pulling your right arm up…*
  - *…and down*
- *Your left arm up.* Continue in this manner until all body parts have been gently raised or moved. Be sure to raise unusual parts, such as elbows, wrists, left ear, and so on.
- *Now I am going to pull several strings at once and you will sit up—carefully. I haven't lifted your head yet.*
  - *Now your head.* Continue as long as desired or until students tire.
- *Feel your strange body.*
  - *It is being held up only by strings.*
  - *Now I am very gently wiggling the strings.*
  - *You stay seated, but your body moves in tiny wiggles—all over.*
- *Now I'm going to cut the strings and you will all gently drop back to your desk—when I tell you. NOW!*

Debrief: *Tell a neighbor what it felt like to be moved by a puppeteer.*

34. The Big Yawn

Objective: To "fake" yawning and stretching with as much reality as possible.

- *Sit comfortably, feet on floor.*
- *Listen to my voice. You are feeling very tired*
- *You need to yawn. Go ahead—yawn.*
- *Bigger, bigger…keep yawning and watch your neighbors as you yawn.*
- Since yawning is contagious, if the teacher can also yawn (or fake a yawn) this helps. By inviting students to watch others yawn, eventually some will actually be yawning.
- Then encourage further: *Now add stretches to your yawns. Big, huge, long stretches. Stretch every part of you body. Make no noise—just stretch and yawn.*

Debrief: This is a good one to debrief as students will be interested in the contagious effect of stretching and yawning. Examine how they felt having to follow instructions and perform artificially something that is usually automatic.

Showcase: Some students *love* sharing their amazing yawn/stretch combinations.

Get Moving

Subjects: Science; Social Studies
Individual

Note: Remind students that they are to remain quiet throughout, and to concentrate on their own actions.

35. Glass Blower

Objective: To imagine blowing glass into something beautiful.

- *Sit quietly, feet on floor, hands on desk.*
- *You are going to be a glass blower. On your desk there is a lump of soft glass.*
  - *Pick it up. Feel it. It's like squishy clay.*
- *Now make your hands into gentle fists and place them to your mouth as if they were a long blowing tube.* Demonstrate: put the thumb side of one fist to the mouth, and the thumb side of the other behind it to form a hollow "tube."
- *Your glass lump is attached to the end of your tube. Now you are going to blow gently through your hands and the glass will start to take form. Blow gently; if you blow too hard, you will destroy the glass.*
- *Concentrate on what you are making with your glass. Are you making a vase? A glass animal? A beautiful ornament? A crystal ball? Look at it as you blow—slowly—carefully.*
- Keep cueing them like this for 30 to 60 seconds.
- *Now your item is complete. You will very carefully put your tube down by releasing your hands, and gently remove the object from the end. Careful. It's warm; it's very delicate.*
- *Set it on your desk and look at it. Isn't it beautiful?*
  - *Look at all the detail.*
  - *Memorize what it looks like.*
- *You made this by being calm and gentle.*

Showcase: Students, in turn, quickly tell what they "created."

Get Moving

Subject: Science
Individual

36. Levitating Arms

Objective: To experience the unusual feeling of arms raising on their own.

- *Sit tall, hands on desktops, feet flat on floor.*
- *You are going to spread your arms a little wider than your shoulders and press your hands firmly down to the tops of the desks.* Model this on teacher's desk; press the entire palm down.
- *Now you try. Keep pushing until I say stop.* Wait for 60 seconds; continually encourage them to keep pushing.
- *When I tell you to stop, just let your arms float into the air. STOP!* Model floating your arms.
- *What happened? How do your arms feel?* They will feel light, almost weightless, depending on how much pressure was exerted and how long the pressure was held.
- *Now we'll try it another way. Put the palm of one hand on the back of the other. Push up with the bottom hand and down with the top one. Hold the pressure until I tell you to stop.* Continue up to 60 seconds.
- *Let go and let the bottom hand rise up. Same feeling?*

Debrief: It is important to allow a few minutes to discuss probable reasons for this strange feeling. Ask students what the experience felt like, and why they thought it felt this way. This is a very brief motivator and a quick debriefing can easily fit within the three-minute time frame.

Extended Debrief: A good extension of this is descriptive writing.

Get Moving

Subjects: Health & Wellness; Phys Ed

Individual

37. Life Rhythms

Objective: To connect speed of tapping with different life emotions.

- *Sit straight in your desk, feet on the floor, eyes on me.*
- *We are going to tap our desks with fingers (or clap our hands) either very slowly, a little faster, or very quickly, depending on the cues I give you.* Model very slow taps, then very quick taps.
- *Some feelings or emotions feel like they slow us down—like fear, for instance. It might tap slowly.* Model and let students copy. *But excitement would be very fast.* Model and let students copy.
- *Some feelings might be very soft taps, while others might be hard taps. It's up to you to choose. I might choose soft and slow for a feeling like worry.*
- *Now I will say an emotion and you will tap the speed you think best describes that feeling. This is not a contest—everyone might tap different speeds, and that's okay. Just tap for yourself and keep the speed you choose until I say a different emotion.*

Debrief: It might be a good idea to briefly discuss the correlation between the rhythms the students tapped and the rhythm of their hearts. This could lead to a lesson on how we handle emotions and, therefore, protect our hearts.

Get Moving

Subject: Science

Individual as part of Whole Class

38. Thunderstorm

Objective: To create the sounds of a storm using the hands and feet.

- *Sit straight in your desk, feet on the floor, eyes on me.*
- *We are going to create a thunderstorm right here in the class.*
- *Begin by rubbing your palms together.* Continue for about 10 seconds. *This is the wind.*
- *Now change to finger snapping.* Continue for about 10 seconds. *The rain.*
- *Now clap—the rain getting harder*
- *Keep clapping and add feet stamping—harder rain and thunder. Harder! HARDER!*
- Continue for no more than 20 seconds, then reverse the sequence.
- *Thunder has stopped!*
- *Rain is lessening. Gentle rain.* Snapping gets slower and lighter.
- *Wind turns to breeze.* Progress from quickly rubbing hands together to slowly rubbing and eventually stopping.
- *Listen to the silence following the storm.* Allow 30 seconds of silent listening.

39. Cold–Hot–Not

Objective: To make instant decisions about whether something is cold, hot, or neither.

- *This is a fast-thinking game. If I call out something, like "ice," that is cold, you shout "COLD."*
- *If I call something like "fire," you shout "HOT."*
- *If I call something like "coffee" that can be either, you shout "NOT."*
- *You have to pay close attention and think quickly.*
- Remind the students that not all will respond in the same way, and that's okay. For example, for the word "opera," the teacher might respond "Hot" if she likes opera, while students might respond "Cold" if they dislike it.
- With younger children, use concrete words. With older children, increase the difficulty by using more abstract words, and explaining that their responses depend on how they feel about the item or situation.

* * *

Concrete Words

- Winter, fall, spring, summer, sun, moon
- Niagara Falls, Pacific Ocean, Arctic Sea
- Sauna, shower, swimming pool, bathtub
- Foods; e.g., ice cream, spaghetti, soup, hot chocolate
- Campfire, candle flame, oven, freezer
- Steam, smoke, tornado, hurricane

Abstract Concepts

- Homework, housework, chores
- Any school subject
- Friends, enemies, family, relatives, teachers, coaches
- Kinds of music; e.g., rap, hip-hop, classical, country, rock, pop
- Current TV shows or movies
- Current TV or movie stars, athletes, famous people
- Clothing fads or name brands; e.g., Adidas, Nike
- Popular fast food; e.g., hamburgers, tacos, milkshakes
- Familiar activities; e.g., going to the movies, going skating, talking on the phone
- Popular technology; e.g., MP3 player, camera cell phone, PDA
- Hairstyles; e.g., ponytail, buzz cut, brightly colored hair, Mohawk, dreadlocks, shaved head

Get Moving

Subject: Science

Individual

40. Stuck!

Objective: To experience being "stuck" to the desk.

- *Sit comfortably in your desk, feet on the floor.*
- *Stretch your arms across the desk and put your head down on the desk.*
- *Get as comfortable as possible, with as much of your body touching the desktop as possible.*
- *Listen carefully. When I give you the cue, you are suddenly going to be completely stuck to your desk.*
- *Your feet will be stuck to the floor.*
- *You will need to listen for my cues before you'll be able to get unstuck.*
- *Cue. You are totally stuck. You can't lift anything.*
  - *Try to lift your head. Impossible!*
- *Try each arm—stuck fast!*
- *For the next few seconds you will try unsuccessfully to lift different parts of your body, but you are too tightly stuck.* Wait for about 15 seconds. If any student succeeds in "lifting" a body part, just remind them all that they are too stuck to move.
- *Feel the heaviness of your head stuck to the desk.*
- *Feel the weight of your arms… hands… legs. You might be able to move your knees, but your feet don't move at all.*
- *Continue in this manner for up to two minutes.*
- *The glue is starting to weaken. You can lift one hand…one arm…* Continue giving "unstuck" cues until students are sitting upright again.
- *One final thing is stuck—your backside. You are stuck to your seat and will stay that way until the end of the lesson on _____.*

Debrief: Ask how many students actually had a sense of being stuck. You may wish to discuss possible reason for this.

Get Moving

Subject: **Any as source of statements**

Individual

Props: True/False sentences from any subject area. Teachers can make these up on the spot or select from a previously prepared bank of statements.

41. False Freeze

Objective: To stand up or sit down according to whether or not what the teacher says is true; to "freeze" if a statement is false.

- *Sit sideways in your chair so that you can stand up easily and quickly without bumping anyone else.*
- *You are going to stand up, sit down, or freeze every time I say something.*
- *If I say something that is true, like "I am your teacher," and you are sitting as you are now, you must stand up quickly. True statements require you to move, to change position.*
- *If next I say something false, like "I am a car," you must freeze. In other words, stay standing, don't move at all. False statements require you to freeze.*
- *Then, if I say, "You are students"—that's true—you move again, and sit back down.*
- *So you MOVE every time I say something true. If I say something not true, you FREEZE where you are.*

- Provide sentences slowly at first; gradually increase speed so that students are really moving. This sounds easier than it is. Kids love it, and teachers can review basic subject concepts readily.

Extended Debrief: Statements with "debatable" or "sometimes" responses can lead to effective discussions and writing tasks.

* * *

T/F Samples

- Boys are usually taller than girls.
- Ice melts when heated.
- The sky can be orange.
- Birds fly.
- Dogs meow.
- Chocolate is always brown.
- Blueberries are purple.
- Applesauce is made from pears.
- Erasers remove ink
- Cows drink milk.
- Coffee is always hot.
- A pencil is made of wood.
- Teachers are always female.
- The gym is used for assemblies.
- Ink is blue.
- Cell phones hurt your eyes.
- Video games are always good for you.

Another way to use False Freeze is with rhyming (move) and non-rhyming (freeze) words.

Rhyming	Non-rhyming
See, be, tree, he, free, knee	See, saw
Look, cook, book, nook, took	Tree, trunk
May, hay, stay, okay, yay	Lay, lie
Run, sun, gun, fun, begun, done	Call, hail
Rain, pain, vein, train	Rub, tarp
Fool, school, rule, cool, tool	What, where
Caught, ought, taught	Catch, call
You, do, to, blue, shoe, flew	Bird, wing
Green, seen, been, sheen, keen	Cook, cake
Yet, pet, net, get, met, set, let	Mom, dad
Friend, end, send, lend, depend	Note, nice
Girl, pearl, swirl, twirl	Girl, all
Boy, toy, joy, annoy, ploy	Boy, ball
Pick, stick, nick, quick, sick, picnic	Ill, ail
Teeth, beneath, wreath	Tooth, tough
Ape, gape, grape, tape	Fruit, freckle
Late, gate, plate, date, debate	Dad, bag
Grab, crab, lab, dab, flab, nab	Bought, bring
Ring, sing, bring, thing	Song, sing

Get Moving

Subject: Math (probability)
Individual

Props: A coin, pencil and paper

42. Heads or Tails

Objective: To select Heads or Tails ten times and check your luck.

- *On your paper, write the numbers 1 to 10, in a vertical column.*
- *Now choose Heads or Tail ten times; write "H" or "T" beside each number.*
- *I will toss the coin and you will be checking your guesses.*
- *If you have* Heads *written beside the number, you must stand up before I toss. In this way we'll all know who guessed right for each number.*
- *Stand if you have* Heads *beside number one. Toss the coin; tell students who obviously have the correct "H" or "T" to give themselves a checkmark beside that number.*
- *Continue for all tem numbers, then check for winners; i.e., whoever guessed correctly the most times. If too many are winners the first time through, play the winners off against each other and invite the non-players to take turns tossing the coin.*

Get Moving

Subjects: Science; Language Arts
Individual

43. Ice Cube

Objective: To experience (in the mind) the feeling of having an ice cube dropped down your back.

- *Sit tall in your desk, feet on the floor, eyes on me.*
- *Something is going to happen to you—but in your imagination, in your mind. It may be something that has already happened to some of you.*
- *When I give the cue, a big, cold, ice cube will be dropped down your back.*
- *You won't be able to sit still—you'll have to wiggle or do whatever you can to get it out.*
- *But you won't be able to get it out until I give the Stop cue. At that time, the ice cube will be completely melted.*
- *You might need to stand up, but you can't leave your desk area.*
- *Cue to start; continue side coaching for up to a minute.*

Debrief: *Could you really* feel *the ice melting in your shirt? What did it feel like? Tell a neighbor.*

Showcase: If any students were particularly interesting or amusing, invite them to share.

Get Moving

Subject: Math
Partners

Note: No oral communication allowed.

44. Number Shakes

Objective: To achieve a specific number by shaking fists and extending fingers.

- *Turn to face your partner (your neighbor, the person behind you, etc..)*
- *Sit comfortably with your feet on the floor.*
- *This is like the game Rock, Paper, Scissors. You shake your fists three times and, on the fourth time, you both open your hands at the same time. But instead of making the sign for rock, paper, or scissors, you will hold out as many fingers as you want.*
- *I will call a number and your goal is to try to shake the number I call.*

- *For example, if I call 3, then one partner would need one finger and the other would need two.*
- *Or one partner might shake no fingers (that is, keep the fist closed), while the partner puts out three.*
- *Keep track of how many tries you and your partner need to reach the magic number. As soon as you get the number, raise your hands.*
- This gets a bit competitive, as pairs all want to be the first to get the number. You can play this up or not, depending on your students. It's usually a good idea to stop when several pairs get the number, then start again with a new number. Bigger numbers can involve using all four hands.
- To increase the difficulty level for older students, try positive and negative integers. One partner is positive, the other negative; they must come up with the called number. Or use with subtraction (subtract one number from another to get the called number), multiplication, or even division. Lots of variables are possible.
- Another alternative is to challenge two or more students to shake exactly the same number. In other words, how many tries does it take for both to shake, for example, threes?

Get Moving

Subject: **Math**

Partners

Props: Pencil and paper

Note: No oral communication allowed.

45. Lucky Hi/Lo

Objective: To test luck by trying to match the high or low called by the teacher.

- This is like Number Shakes (page 45) in that it follows the Rock, Paper, Scissors process of shaking closed fists three times and opening on the fourth shake.
- *Begin by writing your name and your partner's name side by side on a piece of paper. Use a little part of your notebook if you like.* (You can supply scrap paper, as long as the distribution doesn't take long.)
- *Sit facing your partner, feet on the floor.*
- *Make fists, and shake three times. On the fourth shake you will open your fists to hold out any number of fingers out you choose.* Allow a couple of practices.
- *Now comes the game part. After you open your fists, I will be calling "High" or "Low." The person whose fingers match the what I call gets a point under his or her name.* Model by using both of your hands. Hold up one finger on one hand and three on the other and demonstrate which hand is high and which is low.
- *If you both show the same number, neither of you gets the point.*
- *To make it fair, I won't watch you as you open your fists.* Turn away but do the "One, two, three" count with them, then say either "High" or "Low." Make the calling random. Avoid just alternating, as students will be quick to pick up on this.

46. Monkey See, Monkey Do

Objective: To create a sequence of interesting arm and hand movements.

- *Turn to face your partner.*
- *Sit straight in your chairs, feet on floor, arms resting on desktops.*
- *Decide who's A and who's B.*
- *Partner A will do an arm or hand movement, something simple like this.* Model opening and closing hands twice quickly.
- *Partner B will copy the movement, then add another movement, like this.* Model opening/closing hands twice, then quietly clapping three times.
- *You will keep taking turns adding movements until I give you the Stop cue.*
- *Try to remember all the actions in sequence. After the Stop cue, you and your partner will go through the whole sequence together.*
- *This is a silent activity; no talking, just doing.*

Showcase: This is an activity students love to share. Allow a few pairs (as many as time allows) to demonstrate their complete sequence in unison.

*   *   *

Possible Movements

- Snap fingers
- Use imaginary lassos
- Tap knuckles together

- Tap desks, knees, forehead, ears
- Shake index fingers
- Make punching moves

Get Moving

Subject: Any

Partners

Note: This is not a silent activity, as it involves students making musical tones. However, these sounds can be omitted entirely and the activity will still be effective.

47. Musical Punching Bags

Objective: To punch imaginary punching bags and attach tones to the punches.

- *Turn to your partner.*
- *Sit with your feet on the floor, facing each other. Make fists*
- *Imagine a small punching bag. It is hanging right in front of you, but not close to your partner.*
- *Take a few practice punches in the air. Remember to stay out of your partner's punching area.*
- *You and your partner are going to take turns punching a bag that hangs between you. It's a small punching bag but, each time you punch it, the bag makes a musical noise of some sort. Remember it's a small bag, so it's a small noise.* Good idea for the teacher to model a couple of musical punches.
- *Take turns with the bag. Try to be creative.* Give cue to start.
- After about 30 to 40 seconds say, *Now take turns copying what your partner did, then adding to that, until you have an interesting combination of punches and sounds.*
- *Pay attention to the most interesting punch-noise combinations you and your partner can come up with. You might be able to share these later.*

Showcase: Invite some pairs to demonstrate punch-sound combinations.

Get Moving

Subject: Science

Partners

Prop: Slow, moving music without words; the activity can also be done without music.

Note: No oral communication allowed.

48. Magic Mirrors

Objective: To mirror the slow, smooth actions of a peer, in mirror image.

- *Turn to face your partner (your neighbor, the person in front of you) and sit up straight with your feet on the floor.*
- *Your job will be to mirror each other's actions. Whatever your partner does with his or her hands and arms, you do exactly the same.*
- *But remember that a mirror shows the opposite, so if your partner is leading and he or she pulls back, you pull back too.* Model with a student.
- *Try to be creative. Make big but very slow movements.*
- *You must maintain eye contact! That's the trick here. Don't look at your partner's hands; look only at the eyes. So MOVE SLOWLY!*
- *If you are the leading partner, you are not trying to trick your partner. You are trying to lead and be followed exactly.*
- *Decide who will be the first leader. Start when the music begins. When I give the signal, change leaders.*
- Give the start cue.
- Allow about 30 seconds, then give the signal to change leaders.

Showcase: This activity lends itself to quickly sharing a sequence of movements with the class; encourage sharing if, and only if, a pair wishes to do so.

Get Moving

Subject: Language Arts

Partners

Props: Pencil and paper

Note: No oral communication allowed.

49. Tap It to Me

Objective: To figure out words by spelling them into a partner's palm.

- *This is a challenge game. You and your partner will challenge the other pairs.*
- *I will give you a word, but only one person in each pair will see it.*
- *That partner will spell it into the palm of the other partner by tapping the correct number of times.*
  - *For example, if the word was* cat, *I'd first tap three times, because C is the third letter of the alphabet. My partner would write down the letter C.*
  - *As soon as my partner writes the letter C, I go on the next letter. I tap once for A.*
  - *My partner writes A.*
- *If my partner guesses the word based on these two letters, he or she can write the whole word. If it's correct, I can go on to the next word, and continue until we have all the words.*
- *If my partner makes a mistake, I shake my head. Remember—NO TALKING!*
- *I will put the words on the board* (Choose two to five words), *so one partner has to turn now so as not to see the board.*
- Difficulty can be determined by your choice of words. It can also be increased by writing a complete short sentence rather than single words.
- *If your partner loses track or you tap the wrong number, moving your hands side-to-side* (Demonstrate) *lets the other person know to start again.*
- Cue to start. Stop when the first pair indicates completion of all words.

50. Shake It!

Objective: To alternate between moving silently and stealthily, and shaking the entire body vigorously on cue.

- *This game is fun because you get to shake your entire body—just like a dog might shake when it's wet.*
- *But you can only shake everything when I say "Shake it!"*
- *The rest of the time, you will shake only the body part I call out.*
- *When I give the Start cue, please stand and walk carefully around the room, being careful of everyone else's space; stay out of each other's "bubbles."*
- Cue to begin. Alternate body parts with "Shake it!"

*   *   *

Body Parts

- fingers
- hands
- shoulders
- one foot (leg, arm, knee, elbow)
- head
- nose
- hair
- backside

Act, Don't Speak

It is inevitable that, with many students moving at the same time, they need to be reminded not to infringe on others. The idea of a personal-space bubble is one numerous teachers use. It refers to the imaginary sphere that surrounds and encapsulates every student. Appreciation of the "bubbles" of peers seems to be a concept readily understood and accepted by children of all ages.

The 3-Minute Motivators in this section require moderate physical involvement on the part of the students. The activities will require them to stand beside or behind their desks and move in some fanciful manner, either alone or with others (i.e., in partners or small groups). In some cases they will actually move around the room. However, these are silent refocusers; no talk is allowed; this helps to control any heightened energy that may accompany the activities.

The very nature of these motivators makes them excellent for very active children who need to burn off a bit of energy before more focused seatwork or a listening activity. Older students (up to and including high school) still benefit from getting up and moving when they start to feel or act bored or sleepy.

Because the students are acting or doing, they are, in fact, representing. They are also listening closely to cues from the teacher. Short-term memory and imagination, as well as cognition, come into play as students engage in the various activities. If showcasing is involved, instant visualization is added to the repertoire of areas being addressed.

- Most students enjoy these more active exploits. However, if a student is shy, challenged in any way, or just feeling "out of it," it's a good idea to promote the use of the Pass—the right to "sit this one out as long as you refocus with everyone else when it's over."
- Remember to reinforce the silent nature of these activities; often the fun is greater simply because no *oral* communication is allowed.

Act, Don't Speak

Subjects: Phys Ed; Health & Wellness

Individual

51. Fast Feet

Objective: To provide an escape for excess energy by quickly, silently "running" feet.

- *Stand quietly beside your desk. Remember to stay in your own space bubble.*
- *When I give the Start cue, you will quickly and quietly run on the spot. You will move your feet as fast as possible for five seconds. Then, on cue, stop the fast feet and change to slow, silent marching on the spot.*
- *During the fast-feet portion, bend over slightly.*
- *During the slow-march portion, stand as tall as possible.*
- Continue alternating fast feet/slow march—five seconds each, for up to two minutes. Model how to move feet very quickly without noise or forward movement.

Act, Don't Speak

Subject: Science

Individual

52. Melt

Objective: To melt into nothing, as a candle or snowman would.

- *Stand beside your desk.*
- *Stand as tall as possible. You are a snowman (candle).*
- *When I give the Start cue, you will start to melt. Remember to melt from the top down—very, very slowly.*
- *See if you can take a full 60 seconds to melt into a puddle on the floor. I will tell you as the time passes.*
- Cue to start.
- Tell students when each 10 seconds have passed.
- Once they are on the floor, say, *Now you are just a puddle of water (of wax). Relax. Don't move. When I give the cue you will return to sitting in your desk.*

Debrief: *What did it feel like? Share with a neighbor.*

Showcase: If any students were particularly interesting, invite them to share.

53. Balancing Act

Objective: To balance in various positions.

- *For this game you will need to stand quietly beside your desk.*
- *I will ask you to balance in some different ways.*
- *Listen carefully and hold the balance once you get it.*
- *A good tip is to look at a spot on the floor about one body-length in front of you. Focus on that imaginary spot, and it will be easier to keep your balance.*
- *You will be competing with yourself; try to increase the time you can hold a position each time we do it.*
- *If you lose your balance, take a breath and re-balance.*
- Have students hold each balance, beginning with 15 seconds and working up to 60 seconds.
- Challenge students to come up with other balance poses.

* * *

Use your judgment as to the difficulty of the balances you have them attempt. The following balances are listed in order of difficulty, from easiest to most challenging:

1. Simple Stork: one leg on other knee; arms out to sides
2. Complex Stork: one leg on knee; hands clasped above head
3. Simple Skater: one leg extended behind; arms to sides
4. Harder Skater: one leg extended behind; arms pushed out in front, hands clasped
5. Complex Skater: one leg extended behind; arms tightly presses to sides
6. Simple Pretzel: one leg behind, foot held with opposite hand (i.e., right hand holds left foot); other arm out straight
7. Complex Pretzel: Same as Simple Pretzel, but with other arm behind back
8. Easy Squat: Squat down with one leg extended in front, arms wide
9. Complex Squat: Same as Easy Squat but with arms behind back

54. Bump on the Head

Objective: To be a nail or a screw and experience being pounded or screwed into a piece of wood.

- *Stand quietly beside your desk.*
- *When I give the Start cue, you will become a huge nail (screw).*
- *Then every time I give the cue (clap my hands, etc.) a huge hammer (screwdriver) will hit you on the head (turn you) and push you a little further into the ground.*
- *Remember that your feet will be the first to disappear, then a little more with each bang.*
- *You'll end up squatting as close to the floor as possible. It will take about ten hits (turns) for this.*

Act, Don't Speak

Subjects: Music; Language Arts

Individual as part of Whole Class

55. Knocking Knees

Objective: To maintain a continually expanding sequence of clap/knee actions.

- *For this game you must turn sideways in your chairs.*
- *We are going to keep a rhythm using just our hands and knees.*
- *I'll start you off.*
- *Then I'll call a name, and that person will add another movement to the sequence. We'll keep building until we can't remember anymore.*
- *If I call your name and you can't think of anything, just say "Pass."*
- *Let's start with this:* Clap hands once, hit knees twice.
- Repeat this sequence a few times before calling on a student.

* * *

Suggested Movements

- Bump knees together two or three times
- Click fingers and lift knees alternately
- Open and shut knees several times
- Clap hands on or under knees
- Stamp feet: stamp in/out/in/out, front/back, etc.
- Hit opposite knees; i.e. right hand to left knee, left hand to right knee
- Clap to the side, above, behind backs, far out in front

Act, Don't Speak

Subject: Any

Individual

56. Wide–Hide

Objective: To move rapidly from a standing, wide stance to a curled-up, hiding position.

- *First we will stand beside the desks and try to take up as much room as possible without moving.*
- *Spread your arms; stand wide like you are hugging a huge ball.*
- *Now, quickly go from that Wide position—an embracing or welcoming position—to becoming as small as you can, all curled up as if trying to disappear in your desks. This is your Hide position.*
- *Now sit normally. I will say something.*
  - *If it's something you like or feel good about, immediately get Wide and embrace.*
  - *If it's something you dislike or feel badly about or are afraid of, quickly get into the Hide position and try to be invisible.*
- *There can be no in-between. You have to choose either Wide or Hide.*
- *Remember that everyone will have different reactions. There is no right or wrong answer to any of the suggestions. You may want to hide from all of them, or you may want to get huge and embrace all of them.*

* * *

Suggested Words

- Freezing weather
- Warm sandy beach
- Amusement park
- Pollution
- Foul-smelling garbage dump
- Rocket to space
- Boys/Girls
- Homework

- Ice-cream sundaes
- Brussell sprouts
- Pizza
- Dancing
- Mountain climbing
- Deep-sea diving
- Going to the dentist
- Monster (horror) movies

Act, Don't Speak

Subjects: Phys Ed; Science; Art

Partners

Note: No oral communication allowed.

57. Morphing Madness

Objective: To work with a partner to quietly create, using bodies only, whatever object or being the teacher calls.

- *You and your partner will need to stand together beside your desk, so make sure you have room to move.*
- *This game requires the two of you to use your bodies to make or represent a single thing or being.*
  - *For example, if I call out "Telephone pole," one of you might stand tall while the other stands facing with arms straight out.*
  - *Or you might stand back to back, both of you with arms out to the side.*
- *Try it.*
- After each body morph, invite students to stay in form but to look around at peers.

Showcase: Invite any pairs who were particularly creative to share a specific morph with the class.

* * *

Suggested Morphs

- Bridge, tower, house, door, gate, fence, church
- Elephant, giraffe, frog, turtle, alligator, bird, butterfly
- Beach ball, swing, kite, scissors, footstool, ladder, tub, box
- Rock, tree, waterfall

Act, Don't Speak

Subject: Any

Individual as part of Whole Class

Note: This game is based on Simon Says. It is popular with all ages, and its effect is definitely enhanced with prizes.

58. Do This! Do That!

Objective: To copy only the actions accompanied by the call "Do this": this is an elimination game.

- *Everyone stand up, please.*
- *When I do an action and say "Do this!" you copy the action.*
- *If I do an action and say "Do that!" you* don't *copy me. In fact, if you move even a tiny bit, you will be out and have to sit down.*
- *The last few standing will be the winners.*
- *If you are out early, your job is to carefully watch the standing people for any hints of movement on the "Do that"s.*
- Do a practice run. It may be a good idea to stand on a chair so that students can easily see you as you lead.
- There will probably be time to play more than once in the three-minute time. To change it up, invite students to lead.

Act, Don't Speak

Subject: Health & Wellness

Individual as part of Whole Group

Note: No oral communication allowed.

59. As the Circle Turns

Objective: To move left, right, in, or out while being part of a circle.

- Begin by getting students into either one large group holding hands (dependent on available room), or several smaller groups (no less than four or five students per group) in a part of the room where they can move the circle either way.
- Have them stand holding hands.
- *This is a game that will involve cooperation but no talking.*
- *I will give you movement cues to follow as a group.*
- *For example, I might say, "Two steps to the right," and you'd have to do that as a group.*
- *At first I will give the cues slowly, but they will get faster and faster, so you'll need to listen carefully and work together.*
- *No pushing—just cooperating.*
- The idea is to keep the group moving as quickly as possible without endangering anyone. Use your judgment as you see how students behave.

* * *

Suggested Movement Cues

- Any number of lateral steps to either side
- Any number of steps in or out
- Arm movements, such as "Arms up," "Arms in," "Arms down"
- Foot movements, such as "Left foot off the floor," "Right leg shake in the air"
- Level cues, such as "squat as low as possible," "stand on tiptoes"

60. Lean on Me

Objective: To provide and receive physical support for/from peers.

- *This is a game of trust and cooperation.*
- *I will provide cues from which you will have to figure out a position with your partner.*
- *One partner must always be leaning or using the other for support.*
- *For example, if I say, "Back to back," you will stand back to back, but one partner must lean back against the other for support.*
- *You can talk about it as you find the positions, then hold the position until I give another cue.*
- *You must take turns being the one who is supported.*

Debrief: *Quickly discuss what it felt like to be supported by another.*

Extended Debrief: Students write or talk metaphorically about being supported.

Showcase: Invite pairs to share a few of the more original poses.

* * *

Suggested Position Cues

- Side to side
- Back to side
- Hand to shoulder
- Hand to hand
- One leg off the floor (for one partner; for both partners)
- Foot to hand
- Knee to knee

61. Lump of Clay

Objective: To take turns molding partners into forms.

- *Please stand beside your desk with your partner. Decide who's A and who's B.*
- *When I give the start cue, Partner B will become a very soft lump of clay, and Partner A will become the artist who is going to mold that clay.*
- *Partner B, you must allow A to move your body any way he or she wants to; Partner A, you must protect your clay from hurt or harm, so be careful.*
- *Remember that clay can't talk, so this will be done in silence.*
- *I will know you have created your final piece when A sits down to admire the beautiful artwork.*
- *I will allow you only about two minutes to create your work.*
- *Give Start cue.*
- *After about two minutes, give Stop cue.*
- *If time permits, allow students to change roles and repeat the experience.*

Showcase: Invite students to look around at what others have sculpted.

* * *

Suggested Subjects

- a piece of furniture
- a plant or tree
- a container of some sort
- a telephone pole

Act, Don't Speak

Subjects: Health & Wellness; Language Arts

Partners

62. Ages of Humanity

Objective: To physically experience the rapid aging of a human being.

- *For this game, you and your partner will be two friends who start out life as babies and quickly "fast forward" to become old people.*
- *You will need to listen carefully to my side cues so you know what to do.*
- *Try to work together to really* feel *what happens to yourselves as you get older and older.*
- *You may use the area beside your combined desks, but do not interfere with the areas of others. Remember to respect the spaces bubbles of other pairs.*
- *Every time you hear my cue, you will grow older. Listen carefully for the cue and freeze for a few seconds to hear the next directions.*
- *When I cue you to begin, you are both infants in cribs that are next to each other. You will have to lie on the floor to do this.*
- Cue to start. Continue at regular intervals with the following (or similar) prompts, remembering to cue between ages.
  - *Look at each other. Kick your feet like babies and communicate with each other as babies in cribs might do.*
  - *Now you are crawling on your hands and knees; you are starting to talk.*
  - *Now you are just starting to walk. Lean on each other; take baby steps— stay in your space bubbles.*
  - *Now you are four years old, in play school. Maybe you argue over a toy, maybe you share.*
  - *Now you are ten-year-olds. What are you talking about? How do you behave? You are best friends.*
  - *Now you are teenagers. How do you look? Move? Talk? Carry on a conversation like typical teens.*
  - *Now you are young adults, still good friends. You have chosen careers—perhaps the same, perhaps different. Discuss your jobs with each other. You are tall, confident, strong.*
  - *Now you are middle-aged—feeling a bit tired. What do you talk about? How do you walk? Are you a bit overweight? Are you overworked? How do you feel? Discuss it together.*
  - *Now you are very old, a grandparent. You use a cane to walk. You can't see or hear as well as before. Talk together. What do you talk about?*
  - *Finally, your ages of humanity are over. When I cue you, you will die peacefully by returning to the floor.*

Debrief: Quickly discuss how it felt to fast-forward the aging process.

Extended Debrief: Extended discussion and/or writing at another time.

Showcase: Invite any students to share a specific age.

Words and Movement

The 3-Minute Motivators in this section involve dynamic movements, often away from the desks, as well as verbal interactions. They turn students into controlled "movers and shakers." They all involve students working together; none are done on an individual basis.

At first glance it may seem as if these refocusers might be counterproductive, that they might create chaos rather than reduce it. This is not the case. Because the teacher is in control of the activity, and because actions are completely structured and directed, the ultimate goals of removing excess energy and/or reducing boredom are magically met.

In these activities, all strands of the Language Arts curriculum are covered, often by a single activity. Students are engaged in moving, demonstrating, listening, observing, copying, speaking, and, at times, reading and writing. These 3-Minute Motivators tend to make the best anticipatory sets.

Students need to be reminded about personal space, respect for others, and safety issues. The following quick rules work well.

- Stay in your own bubble.
- Watch out for others, and don't puncture anyone else's bubble.
- Appreciate and respect what everyone is doing. No rights or wrongs.
- Be aware of classroom furniture and obstacles. Move with caution.

Words and Movement

Subjects: Any; Phys Ed

Individual

63. Move It

Objective: To return to desks by moving according to the teacher's directions.

- *First, when I give you the cue to move, you will all walk as far away from your desks as possible, and then stand still. Remember to respect each other's personal spaces.*
- Cue to move away from desks.
- *Now you will return to your desks in an unusual manner. Wait for the Start cue. Remember each other's spaces.*
- *Follow the Move It suggestion as closely as possible.*
- *You can make any sounds you want to accompany the movements, but you cannot use actual words—just sounds.*
- *If students are still restless, repeat the sequence, using a different Move It style.*

Showcase: If a student comes up with a particularly creative move, suggest demonstrating for all to enjoy.

* * *

Move It Suggestions

- Like a spider, kangaroo, monster, snake, rabbit
- Through a thick jungle, forest, slough, rushing river
- On slippery ice, broken glass, hot cinders, rocky slope, deep snow
- Backward
- As if you are very old, are crippled, have broken leg
- Joined to someone else: back to back, hip to hip, elbow to elbow
- Leading with your shoulder, elbow, head, bottom

Words and Movement

Subjects: Any; Phys Ed

Partners

64. Walk This Way

Objective: To duplicate the walk and sound made by a leading partner, and to keep changing "leaders."

- *Turn to your partner (neighbor, friend).*
- *When I give the Start cue, the two of you will stand, one in front of the other.*
- *When I give the cue again, the front person will start to walk and make some funny not-too-loud sound.* Model a march or shuffle accompanied by a soft squeak with each step.
- *The person behind must copy the person in front.*
- *The two of you keep moving like that until you hear the cue again.*
- *Then you both turn around and reverse positions. Now the other person leads, creating a different walk and sound.*
- *You must change leaders every time you hear the cue.*
- *You will move anywhere in the room, as long as you respect the personal spaces (bubbles) of others.*
- *Remember to keep your sounds soft, but creative. Try to use different styles of walking with each change.*

Debrief: Ask students what was funny or interesting about the refocuser.

Showcase: If any pair has demonstrated a particularly interesting walk/sound combination, ask if they would like to share with the class.

Words and Movement

Subjects: Any; Phys Ed

Small Group

65. Wrangle Tangle

Objective: To tangle arms in groups of four or five, then move across the room while tangled.

- Quickly get students into small groups.
- *When I give the Start cue, you will stand in a small, tight circle.* Cue.
- *The goal here is to get tangled up. Each person reach in your right arm and join hands with someone else. You can tangle by going under someone's arm or turning around—whatever.*
- *Now reach in your other arm and tangle up as much as possible.*
- *Now you are in tangled clumps. As a clump, you must think of a sound you will make together. You have ten seconds to come up with a clump sound.*
- *Now, making your clump sound, your tangled clump must move around the room for 30 seconds. If you meet another clump, figure out how to get around it.*
- Cue to start. Allow 30 (or more) seconds. Cue to stop.
- *Untangle—one step at a time—and return to your desks*

Debrief: Discuss the difficulty in moving as a clump. Are there situations in real life where this might happen (e.g., in crowds in subways, malls, airports; in mobs)?

Words and Movement

Subject: Any
Whole Class

Props: One small slip of paper per student in an envelope; several slips marked with an X.

66. Explosion!

Objective: To toss and catch an imaginary ball, and "explode" when an unexpected cue is provided.

- *For this game you will need to stand beside your desks.*
- *I will pass around this envelope. Take a slip, look at it, but keep it secret.*
- *Remember if there was an X on your paper. Hide the paper.*
- *Now I am going to call a name, and throw an imaginary ball to that person. That person must catch the ball, then call another person's name and throw the ball to him or her, and so on.*
- *If you had an X paper, as soon as you catch the ball, shout "EXPLODE!" Everyone has to explode loudly and fall to the floor.*
- *You stay frozen on the floor until I give the "Rise up" cue. Then the person who called "Explode" will toss the ball again.*
- *Remember, only some people can call "Explode." Once a person calls "Explode," he or she cannot call it again. So try to remember who has had the ball and who hasn't.*

Words and Movement

Subject: Any
Whole Class

67. The Old Duke Revisited

Objective: To stand and sit in increasingly rapid succession.

- This is a take off of the popular child's poem:

  The grand Old Duke of York, he had ten thousand men.
  He marched them **up** to the top of the hill and he marched them **down** again.
  And when they were **up**, they were up,
  And when they were **down**, they were down,
  And when they were only **halfway up**, they were neither **up** nor **down**.

The students stand up or sit down when each of the words in bold are sung, holding themselves halfway up on the last line, then standing, then sitting.

- Change the words according to the following example:

  Miss Manson's Grade 3 class were restless once again,
  So she marched them **up** to the top of the hill and she marched them **down** again.
  And when they were **up**, they were up,
  And when they were **down**, they were down,
  And when they were only **halfway up**, they were neither **up** nor **down**.

- *This is an action poem.*
- *First I say a line, then you repeat it.* Recite the entire poem without actions.
- *Now we move up or down on the up or down words. Let's try it slowly.* Practice at least once slowly.
- *Now more quickly!* Continue to increase the speed with each repetition.

Words and Movement

Subject: Any

Whole Class

68. Meet and Greet

Objective: To walk around, greeting peers in as many unusual ways as possible.

- *When I give you the Start cue, you job will be to move freely around the room, greeting as many people as you can in two minutes.*
- *But there's a catch! You must find unusual ways to greet each other. You cannot rely on "Hi" and a wave. You must be creative.*
  - *You might say "Yo!" or "Dude!" or even make up a nonsense word for hello.*
  - *You might touch fists in greeting, or rub shoulders, or bow, or wiggle fingers. Be creative.*
- *You can keep changing the way you greet others, or stay with one way. You decide.*
- Cue to start, then watch for innovative greetings for showcasing.

Showcase: Invite students who greeted or responded to greetings creatively to share what they did.

Words and Movement

Subjects: Social Studies; Literature

Whole Class

69. Mad Milling

Objective: To move around the room in the persona of various characters.

- *When I give the Start cue, move to _____.* Indicate an open area of the room, or suggest moving carefully around furniture.
- *You will be milling. That means walking around, not touching anyone or interfering with their space.*
- *But the fun is that you will be listening to my suggestions and walking according to them.*
- *You can also make any sounds that might accompany specific movements.*
  - *For example, if I said "Walk on hot coals," you might lift your feet quickly and say, "Ouch! Ouch!"*
- *When you hear the cue again, freeze and wait for the next suggestion.*

Extended Debrief: Challenge students to choose one form of movement and expand on it in writing; e.g., a story about a protagonist who moves that way.

Showcase: Invite students to demonstrate various movement strategies.

* * *

Suggested Movements

Walking on

- Ice
- Broken glass
- Eggs
- Soft fur

Walking through/in

- Deep water
- Mud
- Tall grasses
- Snakes

Walking as a

- Very old person
- Marionette
- Toy soldier
- Injured warrior
- Ninja

Walking while feeling

- Tired
- Extremely happy
- Cold
- Afraid
- Sick

Words and Movement
Subject: Any
Partners or Small Group

70. Kodak Moments

Objective: To spontaneously create and hold perfect poses.

- *You've probably heard of a Kodak moment. It means a picture-perfect moment, a time when people are perfectly posed to have their photo taken.*
- *You and your partner (group) will have 60 seconds to create and hold a perfect Kodak moment.*
- *But here's where the fun comes in. I will tell you who you will be portraying before you arrange the pose.*
- *You can discuss the Kodak moment with your partners, but you need to move very quickly. I'll tell you when the first 30 seconds is up.*
- *Let's see who can come up with the most creative poses.*
- *You will be working beside your desks (in the space at the back of the room, etc.). Remember not to move into the space of another pair (group).*
- *Once you have your pose, hold it—freeze it.*
- Begin cueing.

Extended Debrief: Challenge students to write (a story, a new article, a journal entry, etc.) about the people in the Kodak moment.

Showcase: Invite students to look around at the Kodak moments of others before unfreezing them and/or moving to a new moment.

* * *

Suggestions for Kodak Moments

- Family of teddy bears
- Group of superheroes
- Millionaire family
- Family of supermodels
- Family of hillbillies (or any geographically based group)
- Group of ballet dancers (or other kind of dancers)
- Group of preschoolers
- Group of angry mobsters
- Group of nuns and priests
- Members of a team (soccer, basketball, football)

4

Let's Communicate

These motivators work well at times when the class is fidgety but not focusing, when they are restless and not directing their thoughts to the lesson at hand: for example, following a video, story-reading, or Fine Arts class; and before a more focused literacy task, such as writing, or cognitive class, such as Math.

Single Words and Sounds

The motivators in this section require peer cooperation; in many cases students will be fast-talking in some manner with neighbors or nearby small groups. At other times, they will be making appropriate sounds to accompany actions. For the most part, these motivators involve individuals conversing or communicating within the protective confines of the entire group. They are completely independent, but still collective, activities that culminate in magical minutes of sound making.

These motivators involve considerable cognition and creativity, as well as short-term memory. In addition, they encourage social constructivism, or learning from peers, making them excellent for diverse classrooms where some students may be less fluent with the language or less capable communicatively, thus benefitting from peer interaction.

- In these activities, basic literacy skills come into play in an entertaining, motivating, and almost magical manner—plus talking is allowed and encouraged within the limitations of the activity. How much fun is that?
- Many of these 3-Minute Motivators benefit from debriefing.
- Many of the activities in this section lead beautifully into further individual tasks, such as writing or researching.

Single Words and Sounds

Subject: Any

Individual as part of Whole Class

71. Talk-a-lot

Objective: To talk non-stop about anything for a full 60 seconds.

- This activity works best when students have been excessively chatty, as it beats them at their own game.
- *It seems you all need some talk time. Okay, you have exactly one minute to talk.*
- *You must talk for a whole minute, but when I give the Stop cue, you must stop immediately and face me.*
- *Remember—everyone must talk when I say, "Go." Everyone will be talking at the same time. Get all you have to say said in one minute. You'll be surprised how long a minute can be.*
- *GO!*
- I have never had students continue talking after the Stop cue. They are so amazed that you invited them to talk that they readily adhere to the limits.

Single Words and Sounds

Subjects: Language Arts; Any as source of words

Individual

72. Interactive Words

Objective: To chant words as they are broken into pieces.

- Write a fairly lengthy word on the board.
- Invite students: *Say after me.*
- This is a chanting activity. Begin saying the word repeatedly, each time dropping a single letter from the beginning:

  - *SPAGHETTI*
  - *PAGHETTI*
  - *AGHETTI*
  - *GHETTI*
  - *HETTI*
  - *ETTI*
  - *TTI*
  - *TI*
  - *I*

- After you have modelled, write other words and invite various students to lead the chant.
- Choosing words from core curriculum (e.g., equilateral, dinosaur) is a way to reinforce vocabulary, spelling, phonetic awareness, and fun!

Single Words and Sounds

Subject: Language Arts (phonetic awareness)

Individual as part of Whole Class

Prop: Short reading selection

73. Oscar

Objective: To say "Oscar" every time a word or sound is heard.

- *Sit comfortably in your desks, feet on the floor, facing me. Don't slouch, because you will need to be very alert!*
- *I am going to read from _____ (name the text).*
- *Every time you hear the "s" sound at the beginning of a word (–ing ending; word that rhymes with* at, *etc.), you must shout out "OSCAR!"*
- The reading selection can be a picture book, a piece of poetry, a section from a textbook or novel—whatever you wish.
- This activity is a favorite with all ages. The word *Oscar* is an amusing and easy-to-say word that children enjoy shouting; however, any word can be used.
- If a word from a specific subject (e.g., *isosceles, equilateral, ecosystem, revolution*) needs reinforcing, use that instead of *Oscar*. To increase the difficulty, simply alter what the students must listen for: e.g., *Listen for any words related to ecosystems and shout "Ecosystem!" when you hear one.*

Single Words and Sounds

Subject: Math

Individual as part of Whole Class

74. Count-Off

Objective: To attempt to count as high as possible, one student at a time.

- *Sit comfortably in your desks, feet on the floor, eyes front.*
- *You are going to count as high as possible as a class. Sounds easy doesn't it? How high do you think we can count?* Solicit responses.
- *But here's the tricky part. Anyone can say a number, but if two or more people say the number at the same time, we have to start all over.*
- *You can turn around so that you can see everyone, but remain in your desks. Watch and listen carefully so that no two people speak at the same time.*
- *No more than three seconds can go by between numbers.*
- *Start counting.*
- This is quite challenging. It's difficult to say a number without someone else saying it too. Most groups never get past 5 or 6.

Single Words and Sounds

Subject: Language Arts (phonetic awareness)

Individual as part of Whole Class

75. Hip-hip-hooray

Objective: To combine word parts into wholes and chant three times quickly, like a cheer.

- *This is a game where we all get to shout "Hip-hip-hooray," and throw our arms in the air. Let's try it once!*
- *Now circle your arm three times as if we were shouting "Hip hip hooray" or giving three cheers, such as "Rah! Rah! Rah!"* Model if necessary.
- *I am going to give you a long word, but I will say it all spread out.*
- *Like this: ca-ter-pil-lar.*
- *You will put the sounds together like three cheers. When you've finished, shout "Hip-hip-hooray!" and throw your arms up!*
- *"Ca-ter-pil-lar" will sound like "CATERPILLAR! CATERPILLAR! CATERPILLAR! HIP-HIP-HOORAY!"*

Extended Debrief: If used with older students, ask them to write down a couple of their favorite words and, when the interrupted lesson is complete, discuss what the words mean and use them in sentences.

* * *

Although this is a sound-blending game suitable for young children, it works surprisingly well with older students too, especially if lengthy, interesting words area used. The following suggestions are divided by difficulty.

Easier		More Difficult	
Multiply	Kindergarten	Personification	Serendipity
Family	Paper	Appaloosa	Misdemeanor
Communicate	Happy	Conundrum	Derogatory
Alphabet	City	Cybernetics	Vestibule
Banana	Summer	Monologue	Trajectory
Dinosaur	Winter	Periodical	Precipitate
Woman	Butterfly	Onomatopoeia	Rigmarole
		Objectionable	Personification

Single Words and Sounds

Subjects: Health & Wellness; Language Arts

Individual as part of Whole Class

Prop: Short verses suitable for chanting

76. Chant-along

Objective: To chant simple words/text with peers.

- *Sit straight in your desks, feet on the floor, eyes on me.*
- *Don't lean against the chair backs. Sit tall.*
- *We are going to chant together.*
- If students can read, put the chants on overheads or board. Otherwise, use the "I say, you say" method, and repeat the chant several times until memorization takes place.

Debrief: Invite students to suggest why chanting has a calming effect.

* * *

Suggested Chants

1. Slowly I go, slowly I know, and slowly I grow—Slow! Slow! Slow!
2. I close my eyes, I close my ears. I say good-bye to hurts and fears.
3. The hurry in my head I cease, I fill it up with gentle peace. I close my eyes and beauty see. I deeply breathe, and calm I'll be.
4. One and two and three and four, I'm counting now, peace to restore. Five and six and seven too—relaxing, calming through and through.
5. *Pitter patter* falls the rain, making all seem clean again. Gently, softly falling down, in sparkling puddles all around.

Single Words and Sounds

Subject: Science

Individual as part of Whole Class

77. Animal Farm

Objective: To participate, using animal sounds, in a whole-class animal chorus.

- *We are going to become an animal chorus.*
- Break the class into five or six equal parts (i.e., tables or rows), and assign each group one of the following animals: cows, chickens, ducks, horses, donkeys, pigs, dogs, cats.
- *First we need to practice the sounds these animals make.* Have each group, in unison, make the appropriate sounds.
- *You all know the tune _____.* Choose a familiar melody, such as "Three Blind Mice," "Twinkle, Twinkle Little Star," "Jingle Bells," etc.
- *Now we will make our animal sounds to the melody, starting with one group at a time, and then all together.*
- Begin by having each group sing a line of the melody using the animal sounds; then have the entire group sing together.

Single Words and Sounds

Subject: Language Arts

Individual as part of Whole Class

Prop: An overhead of sentences with punctuation missing (optional).

78. Punctuate This!

Objective: To become punctuation marks for a piece of text or reading.

- On the board or overhead, write a sentence containing a variety of punctuation:
  - e.g., The boy, his face red, shouted, "Where's my ball?"
- *We are going to BE the punctuation for this sentence. Let's think of sounds or actions that will represent each of the punctuation marks.*
- Allow students to be creative. Actions can accompany sounds.
- *Now, each time we need one of these punctuation marks, you will* (make the sound, do the action).
- After a practice run, share sentences with the class, at whatever level the students are working. Encourage verbal and physical interaction with the punctuation marks.
  - e.g., The boy (*squeak*) his face red (*squeak*) shouted (*squeak*) shouted (*squeak; click, click*) Where (*mmmmmm*) s my ball (*wooooo; click, click*)

*   *   *

Suggested Actions

- Period = clap once
- Comma = "Squeak"
- Question mark = "Woooooo"
- Quotation marks = two clicks of fingers
- Exclamation mark = "Bang!"
- Colon = "Beep! Beep!"
- Semicolon = "Beep, Ahhhhh"
- Apostrophe = "Mmmmmmm"

Single Words and Sounds

Subjects: Language Arts; Math; Any as source of themes

Partners

79. Alphabet Pyramid

Objective: To think of words starting with subsequent letters of the alphabet.

- *Sit in your chair facing your partner.*
- *You will take turns speaking.*
- *I will give you something to talk about, but every word you say must begin with the next letter of the alphabet in sequence.*
- *For example, I might start with "apple," then my partner would say "banana," then I could say "cake," and so on.*
- *Here's the catch—your words must build a pyramid.*
  - *So it would go "apple," "banana, banana," "cake, cake, cake," then maybe "donut, donut, donut, donut," and so on.*
- *All the words you say must fit the theme I give you. What theme was I using for the words I just shared?* (Foods)

*   *   *

Suggested Themes

- School
- Summer holidays
- My favorite things
- Brothers or sisters
- Homework
- The forest (mountains, ocean, lake, river…

Single Words and Sounds

Subjects: Science; Any

Individual as part of Whole Class

80. Popcorn

Objective: To make tiny bouncing moves and popping sounds, like popcorn popping.

- *Sit tall in your seat and keep your feet on the floor at all times during this activity.*
- *You are going to be popcorn kernels in a popper.*
- *When I give the Start cue, start popping: bounce up a little on your chairs and make a light "pop" sound each time you bounce.*
- *We will bounce slowly at first—just like when popcorn starts off.*
- *Then we'll gradually get faster and louder as I cue you.*
- *As you pop, try to go from tiny kernel to puffy popcorn.*
- Side cue to increase speed and loudness.

Single Words and Sounds

Subject: Math

Whole Class or Small Group

81. Clap 3

Objective: To maintain an oral sequence of numbers, or counting, but to substitute a clap for every 3 or multiple of 3.

- *This is a counting game. We will start at one side of the room and just keep counting the numbers in sequence.*
- *But here's the challenge! You mustn't say the number 3, OR any multiple of 3. Instead you must clap.*
  - *For example, it would go like this: one, two,* clap, *four, five,* clap, *seven, eight,* clap—*and so on.*
- *Now here's where it gets really exciting. If a number even has a 3 in it, you must clap for the 3:*
  - *For example, for 31 you must do this:* Clap, one
- *There are no winners or losers here. We are working together to see how fast we can count.*
- This can be simplified for younger students by using simpler conditions: e.g., every other person claps; every number with a 2 in it claps.

Single Words and Sounds

Subjects: Language Arts; Math

Partners

82. The Numbered Letter

Objective: To quickly think of a word starting with a specific letter.

- *For this game I will start you off with a word and a number. You and your partner must say words that begin with the letter that comes in the numbered position in the word.*
  - *For example, if I say* school *and 3, you and your partner must say words that begin with the third letter in "school"—the letter* h.
- *The trick is to go as fast as you can.*
- *No repeating, no mumbling or hesitations.*
- *If your partner makes a mistake, then you win the first round. Just start again and keep going until I cue you to stop.*
- Difficulty can be enhanced by placing a theme on the words; e.g., all words must have to do with a core subject unit of study. This works well as vocabulary reinforcement for a specific subject.

Single Words and Sounds

Subject: Any

Individual as part of Whole Class

83. If You're Happy…

Objective: To participate in group exploration of the familiar tune "If You're Happy and You Know It."

- Review the song:

> If you're happy and you know it clap your hands (*clap clap*)
> If you're happy and you know it clap your hands (*clap clap*)
> If you're happy and you know it and you really want to show it.
> If you're happy and you know it clap your hands (*clap clap*)

- *First we have to think of something else we might feel or do, instead of feeling happiness. Invite suggestions.*
- *Now we'll sing the song with our new ideas, and add the actions.*
- *Once we've added a couple of verses, we'll being at the beginning with "happy" and put then all together.*
- *Success of this motivator depends on quickly establishing a couple of other emotions or activities and associated actions.*

*   *   *

Suggested Actions

- Angry: stomp your feet
- Tired: stretch your arms
- Lonely: hug yourself
- Itchy: shake your legs
- Restless: shake your hands
- Leaving: wave good-bye
- Frightened: bite your nails
- Hungry: rub your tummy

Single Words and Sounds

Subject: Any

Individual as part of Whole Class

84. Quick Catch

Objective: To toss and catch an imaginary object.

- *For this game we will need to pay close attention to each other, because we are going to be throwing and catching an imaginary object.*
- *You can decide the object is anything: small ball, a football, a sword, a marble, a paper airplane, a heavy steel ball, a bowling ball, a pencil—whatever you can think of.*
- *First you will need to catch whatever has been thrown to you.*
- *Then you must call the name of the person you are throwing to, and quickly say what you are throwing.*
- *The fun of the game is that we must work cooperatively. That means we have to try to remember who has already been thrown to, and throw to someone else until everyone has had a turn.*
- *Think of what you might throw. Of course you can always throw a ball.*
- *I'll start. I am throwing an egg to _____ (name of student). He will have to catch it carefully, so as not to break it. When he has it he will say, "Got it!" Then he'll call a name and throw something different.*

Debrief: Quickly discuss what was easy or difficult to catch.

Conversation

Conversation activities may well be the most popular 3-Minute Motivators. Students love them; teachers appreciate their refocusing qualities, as well as the inherent learning they provide. In most cases, some form of discourse ensues—often entertaining, even hilarious, dialogue.

For the 3-Minute Motivators this section, students work together, communicating by quickly responding to cues in order to carry on conversations in an unusual or controlled manner. In some cases, the conversations lead to a further activity, such as following a verbal direction with action. In all cases, the dialogues involve quick thinking, careful listening, organizational skills, and communication skills.

These motivators lends themselves to situations where students need to focus on communication of all kinds—media, text, visual—as well as culturally divergent communication forms, dialects, and languages. The tasks invite students to experiment with many varieties of communicative techniques in rapid, fun-filled, concentrated ways.

- These motivators make excellent starting points for all manner of journalling, follow-up writing, and discussing. In fact, many of them leave students with new insights into common everyday situations, as well as a variety of ideas for problem-solving. Quite naturally, these thoughts can become extended lessons.
- Since all these activities involve working with a partner, it may be a good idea to find ways to introduce variety in partners. Rather than always having students pair with the "the person next to you," try "every second person" or "person on the opposite side of the table or row." Just keep in mind that any movement to get to a partner can interfere with the three-minute time limit.

Conversation

Subjects: Language Arts; Music; Social Studies

Partners

85. Song Speak

Objective: To communicate only in song or melody.

- *Sit in your desks, facing your partner, feet on the floor and hands in your laps.*
- *The two of you are going to carry on a conversation entirely in song. You can communicate whatever you want, but you have to sing it.*
- *I will give you a topic to talk about.*
- *Remember to take turns "song speaking."*
- *Model in song. Use a simple tune like "Three Blind Mice" if you don't feel creative.*

  > *All of you,*
  > *Yes, all of you,*
  > *Will talk in song,*
  > *In lovely lovely song,*
  > *About what you did last Saturday,*
  > *Or maybe even Sunday.*
  > *Song/speak about your weekend.*
  > *Start singing now!*

Conversation

Subjects: Health & Wellness; Social Studies

Partners or Small Group

86. I Am You

Objective: To carry on a conversation "in the shoes of" a partner.

- If small groups can be readily formed use them; otherwise, stick to partners for the sake of expediency.
- *You and you partner(s) are going to carry out a discussion, but you must talk as if you actually ARE your partner.* Model by choosing two students:
  - *I am Bobby* (Joan is speaking). *I like playing hockey. I am good at it.*
  - *I am Joan* (Bobby is speaking). *I am good at school work.*
  - (Joan speaking) *Someday I will be a famous hockey star.*
- *I will give you something to talk about. You will discuss what you like and dislike. Maybe even what your pet peeves are, but no put downs—only positive comments. And remember you ARE the other person.*

Extended Debrief: This is a great activity to talk about at length at a later time. Discuss what it felt like having another person talk about you to your face, say good things about you, BE you. Follow up with journalling about anything learned about self.

Conversation

Subjects: Language Arts; Any as source of themes

Partners or Small Group

87. Alphabet Game

Objective: To carry on a conversation in which each sentence begins with the next letter of the alphabet.

- *You need your alphabets for this game.* Refer students to individual alphabets or alphabet on wall.
- *I am going to tell you what to talk about, then you and your partner (group) will discuss the topic. Each person must say a complete sentence. The FIRST word of that sentence will begin with whatever letter comes next in the alphabet.* For example, on the theme of Homework:

  - **A** lot of kids hate homework
  - **B**ut I am not one of those kids.
  - **C**an you tell me why?
  - **D**on't know!
  - **E**very time I get homework, I hate it.

- *If someone can't think of a sentence in a few seconds, that person is out. You could end up with a winner, or you could both get completely through the alphabet.*
- The challenge aspect (competition between players) can be omitted and the game can be entirely cooperative. For younger children, just saying words according to a theme, or making the conversation themeless, can simplify the game.

Debrief: It can be a lot of fun if two students want to face-off before the entire class and attempt the game for all to hear and enjoy. A good choice of themes helps to keep the situation amusing.

Conversation

Subject: Any

Partners

88. Slow-Mo

Objective: To carry on a discussion that continually switches from fast speaking to slow motion.

- *This is a talking game.*
- *You and your partner will talk about a topic that I will provide.*
- *The catch is that you must talk either very quickly—as if someone has put you on fast forward—or very slowly in s-l-o-w m-o-t-i-o-n.*
- *You will change from one to the other every time you hear my cue.*
- *It doesn't matter who is talking when you hear the cue. Just continue the conversation, but change the speed.*
- *Remember—in any good conversation, both people get a change to speak.*
- Cue to begin.
- Cue to change speeds every few seconds.

Showcase: Invite students to share a short dialogue, just for the entertainment value.

Conversation

Subject: Any

Partners

89. A Quantity of Questions

Objective: To carry on a conversation, based on a specific theme, using questions only.

- *Turn to face your partner.*
- *You are going to carry on a conversation about _____.* Provide theme.
- *But the catch is you must speak in questions. For example, if I was talking to my partner about school, the conversation might go like this:*
  Do you like school?
  Do you?
  I think you do, don't you?
  Do you think our teacher is good?
  Are you asking me if I like our teacher?
- *Remember to use only questions. If one of you forgets to use a question, you are both out. Let's see how long you and your partner can last. You need to help each other.*

Debrief: Invite students to share what was difficult about this. If you want to enhance the experience further, invite two volunteers to play-off against each other for the entertainment of all.

*   *   *

Suggested Themes

- Video games
- Sports
- Food
- Clothing and fashion
- TV
- Homework
- Brothers and sisters
- Parents
- Pets

90. You Did What?

Objective: To quickly and spontaneously share with a group three or four sentences about a nonsensical, teacher-supplied topic.

- Quickly get students into groups of four or five, sitting in small circles either at tables or on the floor.
- *I will give you a silly topic, called a "lead statement."*
- *Every lead statement will begin with "What did you do when…"*
- *We will move around the circle, and each person will say the first thing that comes to mind about the topic.*
  - *For example, if the lead statement is, "What did you do when you woke up in the middle of the jungle?" I might say, "I first started to scream. But when I saw some monkeys swinging through the trees, I decided to join them."*
- *First decide who will speak first; I want that person to raise his or her hand to show me.*
- *I might use my Stop cue to change the topic before it gets all the way around the circle, so listen for that.*
- *If anyone wants to use the Pass on a turn for one time around, that's okay. But no more than one Pass per person.*

* * *

Suggested Lead Statements

What did you do when…

…your pet started talking to you?
…you landed on the moon in your newly built space shuttle?
…you opened your closet to find Homer Simpson (or Brad Pitt, Elvis Presley)?
…you looked in the mirror and had no reflection?
…you ate a cookie and suddenly found yourself shrinking?
…you suddenly had the ability to fly (or other superhero power)?

Conversation

Subject: Any

Partners

91. You DON'T Say!

Objective: To carry on a conversation without ever using specific words.

- *This game is a talking game where you must carry on a conversation with your partner, but you cannot use some specific words.*
- *You cannot use "AND" or "I" for this conversation.*
- *If someone uses "and" or "I," that person is out and the other is the winner.*
  - *For example, if I wanted to say "Last night I stayed home and did homework," I'd have to say, "Last night this person stayed home. This person did homework."*
- *If one of you gets out, you can start again if there's time left.*
- *I will tell you what to talk about, and what words you cannot use.*
- *Begin when I give the Start cue.*

Debrief: Quickly discuss how difficult it is to exclude particular small words from dialogue.

* * *

Suggested Words to Eliminate

- The
- And
- My
- I
- But

Suggested Topics

- What you do every morning to get ready for school.
- How you feel about _____ (friends, boy/girl friends, parents, brothers and sisters, homework, school, teachers, curfew)

Conversation

Subjects: Language Arts; Health & Wellness

Partners

92. "Yes, But" Pet Peeves

Objective: To carry on an escalating conversation about pet peeves, in which each speaker has a worse peeve than the previous one.

- *Sit facing your partner.*
- *You are to carry on a back-and-forth conversation for a full two minutes.*
- *You must each start what you say with, "Yes, but…"*
  - *For example, if the starter is "The stars are pretty," the first person might say, "Yes, but they are far away." Then the next person might say, "Yes, but they look closer with a telescope," and so on.*
- *I will tell you what to talk about and provide the opening sentence..*
- *Provide theme and start cue.*

Extended Debrief: *When do we use "Yes, but…" in day-to-day talk? When we use "Yes, but…" what are we saying or doing to what the other person said?*

* * *

Possible Starters

- School is really tough.
- I forgot my lunch today.
- It's raining and we can't have recess
- My dog ran away.
- My mom has to go to work.
- I spent all my allowance on candy.
- My dad got a new car.

Conversation

Subject: Health & Wellness

Partners

93. Glad Game

Objective: To carry on a conversation in which partners complete the sentence beginning "I am glad…"

- *Sit facing your partner.*
- *You are to carry on a back-and-forth conversation for a full two minutes.*
- *You must each start what you say with "I am glad…"*
  - *For example, I might say, "I am glad I am here today," and my partner might say, "I am glad I have my homework done."*
- *What one person says doesn't have to relate to what the other says; you simply have to keep thinking of what you are glad for or about.*
- *You must keep talking until I stop you.*

Extended Debrief: *Recall as many things as possible you said you were glad about, and list them in your journal. Select one to write about further.*

Conversation

Subject: Any

Partners

94. Think Talk

Objective: To keep talking on a teacher-provided subject for a full 60 seconds, without stopping or mumbling.

- *Face your partner and decide who's A and who's B.*
- *When I give the Start cue, Partner A must begin talking—the catch is that I will tell A what to talk about. A must keep talking about that subject until I say "Stop."*
- *Then it will be Partner B's turn, but with a different subject.*
- *You will each talk for a full 60 seconds, without repeating yourself, saying "ah" or "er," stammering, or taking more than two seconds to think. It's harder than it seems.*
- *Now, before we start, raise your hand if you think you'll be able to do this.*
- *If you raised your hand, put a tiny star on your hand (your page). Your partner will judge whether you deserve that star or not.*
- *If you didn't give yourself a star, your partner might decide after you talk that you deserve one.*
- *Let's see how well we know ourselves and our communication abilities.*
- *Any subject-related topic works well with older students, and serves to reinforce learning:*

Debrief: By a raise of hands, check who reached the star goal. Quickly discuss why or why not.

* * *

Suggested General Topics

- Favorite foods
- When I grow up
- Caring for a pet
- Parents and siblings
- Summer holidays

Suggested Subject-related Topics

- Writing an essay
- Doing a science experiment
- Solving a math problem
- Life in an ecosystem
- Making an electrical circuit
- Creating an object from clay

Conversation

Subject: Any

Partners

95. Fortunately/Unfortunately

Objective: To converse with a partner where one person continually begins with "Fortunately," while the other begins with "Unfortunately."

- *Sit facing your partner.*
- *Decide who is A and who is B.*
- *You are to carry on a back-and-forth conversation for a full two minutes.*
- *You must start what you say with "Fortunately" or "Unfortunately."*
- *Partner B will start. B will be "Fortunate." Partner A will be "Unfortunate."*
  - *For example, B might say, "Fortunately today is Friday." Then A could respond, "Unfortunately we have homework for the weekend."*
- *When I cue to switch, you will start your sentences with the opposite word.*
- Cue to start. Continue for about one minute, then switch roles.

Debrief: *Did you learn anything?* There can always be a "fortunate" or an "unfortunate" depending on our outlook.

Extended Debrief: Invite students to create comparison charts for which they think of opposing "fortunates" for any "unfortunates" they may have.

Conversation

Subjects: Health & Wellness; Social Studies

Partners

96. I Appreciate…

Objective: To brainstorm, alternating with a partner, as many appreciated people, things, ideas as possible.

- *Sit comfortably facing your partner (neighbor, friend).*
- *When I give the Start cue, you will take turns saying "I appreciate…" and completing the sentence.*
- Demonstrate; e.g., *I appreciate all my students. I appreciate the fact that my car started today. I appreciate the great lunch I know I packed for myself.*
- Point out that the appreciation can be for abstract concepts as well as actual people, places, or things.
- Cue to start.
- Let the communication continue for up to two minutes, then cue to stop.
- *Now I want each of you to recall one thing your partner appreciated. Tell your partner why your liked that particular appreciation.*

Debrief: Ask students if they learned anything by participating in this activity. (They may have learned that we have lots to appreciate.)

Conversation

Subject: Any

Partners

97. May There Be…

Objective: To discuss possibilities.

- *This is a game of imagining and wishing.*
- *All you have to do is take turns completing the sentence starters "May there be…" or "May there never be…"*
- *Decide who's A and who's B.*
- *Partner B, you will start with "May there be…"*
- *Partner A, you will say "May there never be…"*
- *You will continue this for three sentences each—six sentences altogether. Then you'll switch and A will start with "May there be…"*
  - *What kinds of things might you say? How about "May there be sunshine today." "May there never be a tornado here."*
- *It doesn't matter what you say—just let your imaginations go.*
- *At the end of the talk time, we'll try to recall some of the ideas.*
- *Cue to start.*
- *Stop after a couple of minutes, or when students get bogged down.*

Extended Debrief: Explore the possibility of writing poems based on the ideas students have generated.

Conversation

Subject: Language Arts

Partners or Small Group

98. Third-Person Talk

Objective: To carry on a discussion in third person.

- *This is a curious game of communication.*
- *You will have to talk to your partner about something you will do or have done, BUT you have to speak about yourself in third person.*
  - *In other words, instead of saying "I did…" I would will need to say "Your name did…"Instead of saying "give it to me," I would say "give it to your name."*
- *This is harder than it sounds.*
- *I will give you a topic to discuss.*
- *When I give the Start cue, you must talk for two full minutes in third person.*

Debrief: Quickly discuss what was difficult, and when such a manner of speech might be used.

Extended Debrief: Challenge students to write a story in third person.

Showcase: Invite any pair who seem "natural" at this to share a brief discourse with the class.

* * *

Suggested Topics

- What I did last weekend (or any holiday, time off)
- When I grow up…
- My life with _____ (specific family members)
- When I was younger…
- My first experience with a dentist (or a doctor, hospital, health nurse)

99. Hi-Lo Speak

Objective: To physically be higher or lower than a partner when speaking.

- *I this game, the person who is talking must always be HIGHER than the listener.*
- *For example, if I am talking with Ruth, when I talk, I must be standing raising myself up to be much higher than Ruth.*
- *But when she speaks, even if it's just to say "Yes" or "No," she must be higher than I am.*
- *The idea is that the speaker is always looking down at the listener.*
- *To make it really fun, each person should not talk for long. The shorter your sentence or reply, the more quickly the two of you will have to adjust your positions.*
- *Think of what would happen in a "Yes–No–Yes–No" argument.*
- *When I give the cue, you will begin talking about the subject I will provide, and continue until I cue you to stop.*
- For suggested topics, see Third-Person Talk on page 76.

Debrief: Quickly discuss what was fun or difficult about this.

Extended Debrief: With older students, this lends itself to more in-depth discussions about being higher or lower than others metaphorically.

Brainstorm

Since students will work together to come up with quantities of brainstormed words, ideas, or thoughts, they usually require paper and pencils to record their ideas. Younger students can, of course, also be involved by drawing their ideas, rather than writing them, or sharing them orally with the teacher as they arrive at them.

The 3-Minute Motivators in this section are designed for pair or even team work; they are socially constructive in nature and cover all strands of the Language Arts curriculum. Students will work together to quickly brainstorm ideas based on teacher limitations and suggestions. They might be jotting these ideas on paper, reading them, and sharing them, all in rapid succession. In fact, because these motivators are carried out under time pressure, and because they are generally competitive in nature, they become quite heart-thumping experiences.

These activities engage students in imaginative thought, quick thinking, and rapid recall of information. They are both cognitive and stimulating in nature. Consequently these motivators are great for revving up sleepy brains, for jump starting lethargic imaginations, and for generally engrossing students in an exciting and challenging manner, so that they return to an interrupted topic with renewed vigor.

Some of these refocusers may seem similar to those in the Conversation section; the difference lies in the fact that most of these motivators require only single-word responses, and are done more quickly and spontaneously. Even those requiring more of a sentence or phrase response are of a brainstorming or listing nature.

- Debriefing and extended debriefing can be valuable for the activities in this section, as many of them can be expanded into worthwhile writing, research, or discussion topics.
- Since many of these activities are timed challenges between partners, prizes definitely enhance the fun element. The mere idea of a prize can elevate students' level of commitment.

Brainstorm

Subject: Language Arts
Partners

100. 2-for-10 Tales

Objective: To cooperatively create a ten-sentence story, complete with protagonist, plot, climax etc.

- *Sit facing your partner.*
- *Together you are going to create (write, tell) a story about _____.* Provide theme.
- *But here's the catch. You must use exactly ten sentences!*
- *There are two of you, so that means you have to take turns, and each provide five sentences to make your tale.*
- *And it must make sense. Think of all the things that make a good story and be sure to get them all into exactly ten sentences.*
- *You will have two minutes to complete your story, so you'll have to work quickly.*
- Cue to start.
- After two minutes (or more time if desired), cue to stop.

Debrief: *What was hard about this task?*

Extended Debrief: Invite students to write their stories out in good, sticking to the ten-sentence rule, and participate in whole-class sharing at a later time.

Showcase: Invite a couple of pairs to share their stories. Carefully check for exact number of sentences.

Brainstorm

Subjects: Social Studies; Language Arts
Partners or Small Group

Props: Point-of-View cards

101. Point Please?

Objective: To look at a familiar situation from different points of view.

- *For this game you will need to think in unusual way, but also thing quickly and brainstorm together.*
- *I will give you a situation that is familiar to all of us; for example, "a rainy day."*
- *Your job is to think of as many different ways as possible to look at or think of a rainy day. For example:*
  - *A disappointment for kids going on a picnic*
  - *Great for farmers in a drought*
  - *Good for fish or ducks*
  - *Bad news for people living near a high river*
- *This will be a competition. The group with the most "good" points of view will win.*
- Cue to start.
- Don't allow students more than about two minutes. Keep it snappy.
- Cue to stop.

Debrief: Tally to find a winner, then share these view points with the class.

Extended Debrief: Take the idea of different view points into literature or other subjects (e.g., Social Studies: point of view of displaced persons), and discuss. Or challenge students to write from an unfamiliar point of view.

*   *   *

Make cards with the point-of-view starters like these, so they can be reused:

- Being a victim of a natural disaster: forest fire, flood, earthquake, storm
- Losing something of value: wallet, ID, pet, sentimental jewelry
- The antagonist in a story who steals from the protagonist
- A very hot day on the desert

Brainstorm

Subject: Language Arts

Partners

Note: This game may be too difficult for children younger than about the age of eight.

102. And the Real Meaning Is...

Objective: To brainstorm as many original and humorous meanings of common words as possible.

- *For this game I am going to give you a common word; you and your partner are to brainstorm as many different ways to describe the meaning as you can. For example, if the word was "lazy," you might say*
  - *People who leave their clothes on all night so they don't have to dress in the morning*
  - *A person who lies on top of the bed so he doesn't have to make the bed*
  - *Someone who eats soup out of the can so she doesn't have to wash a pot*
- *You will need to be really creative, maybe even silly.*
- *Remember, you aren't actually giving the definition of the word. You are explaining what the word means when it is used to describe someone or something.*
- *I will give you two minutes to brainstorm ideas and jot them down.*
- *We will share some of the ideas*

Extended Debrief: Use the brainstormed ideas as writing projects, working them into a story or character description.

Showcase: Share a few examples.

*   *   *

Suggested Words

- Happy
- Tired
- Bored
- Compulsive
- Predictable
- Silly
- Workaholic
- Famous
- Infamous
- Evil
- Goodhearted

Brainstorm

Subject: Language Arts; Any

Partners

Props: Pencil and paper

103. Synonym Sense

Objective: To quickly brainstorm synonyms for common words.

- Pair students.
- *I am going to provide a word, and you are to brainstorm together to think of as many other words as you can that mean the same, or almost the same, thing. You will jot down all the words you come up with.*
- *You will have 20 seconds per word.*
- *This is a competition: after two minutes (that is, four words), I will compare your lists to find the winning pair!*
- It's a good idea to do a quick one together as a model:
  - *For the word "Say": speak, utter, talk, chat, verbalize, lecture, address, tell, cry, announce, exclaim, reply, shout, etc.*
- Give the first word. After 20 seconds, cue with the second word, and so on for four words.
- Cue to stop.

* * *

Words with Many Synonyms

- Look
- Happy
- Run
- Ugly

- Fat
- Thin
- Big
- Small

Brainstorm

Subject: Any as source of combinations

Partners

Props: Pencil and paper

104. Go-Togethers

Objective: To quickly think of things that go together.

- *I am going to say the first part of a phrase you are familiar with: "fish and …" What part have I left out? Shout it out.*
- Here are a few more to practice with:
  - *brothers and…*
  - *cats and…*
  - *peaches and…*
- Move to partners. Make sure each pair has a pencil and paper.
- *You and your partner are to quickly think of what's been left off and write it down. See how many you can get.*
- This can be a competition if you like, but it is not necessary. The challenge is inherent.

* * *

There may be appropriate responses that differ the ones offered in parentheses:

Mathematics

- add and (subtract)
- multiply and (divide)
- positive and (negative)

- problem and (solution)
- height and (weight)

General

- peanut butter and (jam)
- pancakes and (syrup)
- cake and (ice cream)
- bread and (butter)
- mothers and (fathers)
- moms and (dads)
- sisters and (brothers)

- grandmothers and (grandfathers)
- keys and (locks)
- shoes and (socks)
- in and (out)
- up and (down)
- north and (south)
- east and (west)

Brainstorm

Subject: Language Arts; Any as source of theme

Partners or Small Group

105. Word Tennis

Objective: To "toss" words rapidly back and forth between partners.

- *Face your partner (or members of your group).*
- *This is a quick-thinking talking game.*
- *I will give you a theme—a big idea—and all the words you say must fit into this theme.*
  - *For example, if the theme is Food, then you could say, "eggs, bread, ice cream…"*
- *The idea is to say a word as quickly as possible. You can't wait more than three seconds or you are out.*
- *If you repeat a word, or say "ah" or "um," you are out.*
- Provide a theme and watch the fun.
- As you note several pairs finish (i.e., with one person out) stop the game and provide another theme.
- A good idea is to use an idea from a current topic in another subject, such as "ecosystems" from Science.
- An alternative is to change "Tennis" to "Association." The students say whatever the previous word makes them think of. For example, "Snow" might lead to "white," to "black," to "witch," and so on. This tends to be a bit more difficult, but equally entertaining and thought-provoking.

Showcase: An entertaining quick conclusion to this activity is to invite any two students to face-off and attempt the game with the class watching.

Brainstorm

Subject: Any

Partners

Props: Pencil and paper

106. Quick Questions

Objective: To brainstorm as many questions as possible for a teacher-presented answer (based on the popular TV show *Jeopardy*).

- *I am going to give you a statement that will serve as an answer.*
- *You and your partner have to think up and write down as many questions as you can for that answer, in a very short length of time.*
  - *For example, if the answer is "The ocean," questions might be "Where do whales live?" or "What is a large body of water called?"*
- Provide an answer and cue to start.
- Keep the pace quick, and compare for number of appropriate questions for each answer.

Brainstorm

Subject: Language Arts

Partners

Props: Pencil and paper

107. Big Word/Small Word

Objective: To quickly morph small words into bigger words.

- *Sit facing your partner (neighbor, friend).*
- *Partner A will say a small word, like "cat."*
- *Partner B has to think of a bigger word that has "cat" in it, like "caterpillar."*
- *As soon as Partner B has the bigger word, B gives A a small word to morph into a big word.*
- *Keep a list of your big and small words as you go.*
- For a simplified version of this game, provide a list of small words and invite partners to brainstorm for bigger words within a time limit. If competition is desired, the pair with the most big words wins.

*   *   *

Suggested Small Words

• in	• ring	• call
• at	• see	• able
• or	• eat	• all
• if	• do	• part
• ill	• but	• no
• got	• with	
• dog	• ate	

Brainstorm

Subject: Any

Partners

Props: Pencil and paper

108. Excuses, Excuses

Objective: To brainstorm more excuses than your partner in a set length of time.

- *This is a great game at which you are all very good.*
- *Sit facing your partner.*
- *When I give the Start cue, you and your partner will brainstorm as many excuses as you can for the situation I will provide.*
- *Jot them down. We'll share some of them later.*
- *Be creative. The excuses can be as wild or silly as you want.*

Extended Debrief: Invite students to choose one very unusual excuse (their own or someone else's) and elaborate it into a story, journal reflection, letter.

Showcase: Share a few of the most creative and humorous excuses.

*   *   *

Suggested Scenarios

- Undone homework
- Late for supper (practice, school)
- Telling of a secret
- Lost books (little sister, pet, pencil, money)
- Broken ornament (TV, video game, glasses)
- Black eye (torn clothes, missing tooth)
- Possession of kitten (puppy, new bike, new hat/jacket/shoes)

Brainstorm

Subject: Language Arts

Partners

Props: Pencil and paper

109. Break-up

Objective: To break large words into as many smaller words as possible.

- *With your partner, you are to make as many small words as you can from the word I provide.*
- *You can use only the letters in the given word as many times as they appear there. So if the word was "apple," then you could use two p's in the words you make. If the word I give is "pear," then you have only one p to use.*
- *You will have three seconds (or up to 60 seconds) to brainstorm and write the new words.*
- *The pair with the most words wins.*
- Use subject-related words to be reinforced: e.g., equilateral, Mesopotamia, equation, geography

* * *

Suggested Words

- multicultural
- extraordinary
- catastrophic
- spaghetti
- pumpernickel

Brainstorm

Subject: Any

Partners

Props: Pencil and paper

110. If They Could Talk

Objective: To brainstorm all the things inanimate objects might say, if they could talk.

- *Take out a piece of paper and something to write with.*
- *You and you partner are going to use your combined imaginations to brainstorm.*
- *I will give you the name of some inanimate object (something without life), and you will think of all the things that object might say if it were alive.*
  - *For example, if I said "apple," you might write, "Please don't eat me," or "I want to be in a pie."*
- *You will have 60 seconds to think. Then we'll share a few of your ideas.*

Extended Debrief: Use the brainstormed ideas as story starters or discussion openers.

Showcase: Share a couple of these, then have students keep them for extended debriefing at a later time.

Brainstorm

Subject: Language Arts

Partners

111. First and Last

Objective: To quickly provide a word that begins with the last letter of the word provided by the previous person or partner.

- *For this game, you will need to concentrate on word spellings.*
- *Your job is to think of a word that starts with the last letter of the word you partner says.*
  - *For example, if I said "father," my partner would have to say a word starting with "r," such as "right." Then I'd say a word that starts with "t," and so on.*
- *You have to think and speak as quickly as possible.*
- *This is a competition between you and your partner. If either of you can't think of a word in two seconds, if you repeat a word, or if you say "ah" or "uh," the other person wins.*
- *I will give you the first word. Cue to start by giving a word.*

5

Beyond the Three-Minute Mark

These motivators also make excellent anticipatory sets. For this reason, a more detailed list of suggested subjects is provided for most of these activities, suggesting curriculum areas where they may work as lesson introductions or anticipatory set.

The activities in this section often *stretch* the 3-minute limit, and have, therefore, been separated. Although these activities may take longer to execute—sometimes up to ten minutes or more—they still work well as refocusers or motivators, as long as teachers debrief in such a way as to return students' focus to the interrupted lesson.

These activities involve the whole class in challenging, enjoyable, and intrinsically motivating activities. These ten-minute motivators involve cognition, short-term memory, all manner of communication, listening, and viewing.

Frequently an element of competition is involved, together with consistently required cooperation. Often two or more students are It; they may be asked to leave the room for a few moments until the class is ready, then return to engage in a mutually entertaining challenge. Students generally *want* to be It. Once they realize the activity is fun, they are eager to be the "main characters."

- Teachers should remind students of the importance of respect, of "no wrong responses," and of demonstrating appreciation for individual efforts.
- I find it helpful to supply small rewards, such as candies, stickers, pencils, erasers, or unusual items from a dollar store for the volunteers who take the leading roles in some of these activities.
- Naturally, students are never forced to be It; however, it is equally important to encourage students to take turns, especially if the same few are always eager to volunteer.

Beyond the Three-Minute Mark

Subject: Any

Partners as part of Whole Class

112. Obstacle Course

Objective: To lead a "blind" partner through an obstacle course of people.

- Begin by dividing the class into two groups. One group (Group O) will be the obstacles, while the other group (Group T) takes the Trust Walks. Halfway through the activity, you can reverse the groups.
- *This game involves trust. You will need to really trust your partner.*
- *Group O, I want you to position yourselves any way you want to, as long as your body presents an obstacle in the room. For example, you might spread your arms and legs into an X, or you might sit down and become a "rock."*
- *Group T, you will have to get past these obstacles from one side of the room to the other. In pairs, decide who's A and who's B.*

- *Partner A, you are the first follower. That means you must shut your eyes during the game, and keep them shut until your partner has led you past the obstacles.*
- *Partner B, you have to carefully lead your partner past the obstacles. You can talk to your partner, guide her or him by the shoulders—whatever. But you must be responsible; don't let your partner get hurt.*
- Allow both groups to experience being both followers and leaders. You may wish to separate this into two activities, rather than have both O and T groups go through the entire experience at once.

Debrief: Quickly discuss how it felt to be leader, follower, and obstacle.

Extended Debrief: Discuss at length various situations in which trust is imperative. This could be extended to a discussion about professions where trust is involved (e.g., police officers).

Beyond the Three-Minute Mark

Curriculum Connections:
Language Arts (grammar, verbs, word choices); Science (importance of using good questioning techniques, especially higher-level thinking questions, when examining data or doing experiments); Math (problem-solving)

Whole Class

113. Let's Quiggle

Objective: To guess, by asking pertinent questions, what activity the class has secretly selected.

- *This is a guessing game.*
- *I need two volunteers to leave the room for about 30 seconds. When they return, they will have to guess what activity, such as "eating," the rest of us have chosen.*
- *The activity will represent an action word, a verb.*
- *The volunteers are It, and will ask Yes/No questions using the word "quiggle" for the activity to be guessed.*
  - *For example, if they ask, "Do you quiggle at home?" we answer, "Yes."*
  - *If they ask "Are you quiggling all the time?" we answer, "No."*
- *They will ask questions until they think they can guess the secret word. They get three guesses.*
- Discuss briefly, or provide another example (e.g., "breathing") until students have the idea. They will note that the secret activity is actually a verb or action word.
- Send the volunteers out of the room. *Okay, we need to think of a good action word that can end in "–ing."*
- Bring volunteers back in and let the fun begin.
- If they are stuck, use leading questions that start with "who," "when," "where," "why," "how." For example, with the verb "eating":
  - *Who do you quiggle with most often?*
  - *When/where/why do you quiggle?*
  - *How do you quiggle?* (The response can be a vague *"with difficulty"* or as specific as *"by using my mouth and teeth."*)
- Or provide more specific clues, such as *"I like to QUIGGLE when I'm hungry."*
- Students quickly get the idea of responding in a more and more revealing manner, so that the volunteers are given more open suggestions. This is a constant work in progress, with learning going on for all.

Beyond the Three-Minute Mark

Curriculum Connections: Science (doing experiments, collecting data); Math (problem-solving); Language Arts (research skills); Health & Wellness (awareness of individuality, that people are more than "what you see")

Small Group

Note: Riddles taken from *Colorful Lateral Thinking Puzzles,* Paul Sloane & Des MacHale. New York, NY: Sterling Publishing

114. Give Me a Clue

Objective: To figure out the answers to riddles, using leading clues provided by the teacher.

- Begin by getting students into groups as quickly as possible.
- *As a group, your job will be to figure out the answers to some riddles.*
- *I will give you clues.*
- *The first group to find the answer wins (gets a point)*
- Present a riddle.
- Present one clue at a time, allowing about 30 seconds group-talk time before presenting the next clue. Continue in this manner.
- If students do not get the answer, provide it fairly quickly so as to maintain the momentum of the game. Use as few or as many riddles as is necessary to refocus or set.
- Any riddles can be used by simply providing a series of consistently more revealing clues.

Debrief: Discuss the importance of looking at all details and thinking in different ways.

Extended Debrief: Challenge students to create their own riddles with clues.

*   *   *

Suggested Riddles

1. What is the only day that doesn't end in a -*y*?
Clues:

- It is the day we all look forward to.
- It arrives many times a week.
- Procrastinators love this day.

Answer: Tomorrow

2. What is unusual about the number 40?
Clues:

- This is not a mathematical property.
- 40 is different from any other number.
- It has to do with order.
- It has a lot to do with spelling.
- It has a lot to do with the alphabet.

Answer: Forty is the only number whose letters are in alphabetical order.

Curriculum Connections: Social Studies (discussions about political platforms, rules and constitution, family connections); Math (problem-solving, fractions); Language Arts (descriptive writing, detailed writing)

Whole Class

115. The Rule Rules!

Objective: To figure out what rule or qualifier students are using when they answer Yes/No questions.

- *For this game, volunteers will guess what rule the rest of the class is using when they answer Yes/No questions.*
- *The rule could be something like, "Every second person must answer No."*
- *Two student volunteers will leave the room. While outside, they should think of two or three simple questions to which responses will be only Yes or No.*
- *The questions should be ones that you already know the correct answers to.*
  - *For example, you might ask "Are you sitting down?" You already know everyone is sitting, so when you get a No answer, that gives you a clue.*
- *The volunteers will ask the same question to several students in sequence and, based on their answers, try to figure out the rule.* Model this with the "Are you sitting down?" question. First person answers Yes, second answers No, third answers Yes, and so on.
- *Volunteers get three guesses at the rule.*
- *If you think of funny questions, like "Are you a monkey?" some students may have to answer Yes, because they will have to follow the rule.*
- *Volunteers please leave.* While they are outside, class decides on a rule.
- Call volunteers back and let them begin. If they are stuck, help them by suggesting a question yourself and quickly asking a number of students so that the rule becomes apparent.
- Initially I let volunteers know which of the three forms of rules— sequence, appearance, or actions—we are using; once the class is familiar with the game, I omit this information and students are still frequently successful.

*   *   *

Suggested Rules based on Physical Appearance

- All those wearing blue (jeans, glasses, sneakers, shorts) answer No.
- All those with curly hair answer Yes.
- All those who have on watches answer No.
- All those with books on their desks answer Yes.

Suggested Rules based on Actions

Answer honestly, and do the following as you answer or before you answer:

- Touch your face
- Cough slightly
- Say "hmmmm"
- Take a big deep breath
- Lean forward
- Lift one foot off the floor
- Scratch your head
- Put your hands together
- Bite your lip
- Look up at the ceiling

Curriculum Connections: Social Studies (how information changes as it is passed along); Math (the importance of accurate renditions of numerals)

Small Group

Props: Pencil and paper; cardstock or paper with simple photocopied designs.

Note: No oral communication allowed.

116. Back Talk

Objective: To copy a design based on tactile impressions put on students' backs.

- Begin by getting students into groups, standing in rows, each person facing the back of the person in front. The front person has a pencil and piece of paper. The back person has a photocopied illustration.
- *This is a game like the telephone game, in which you pass a whisper. But this time you will pass a picture.*
- *No talking.*
- *The person with the picture must draw the first part of the picture on the back of the person in front, using only a finger.*
- *Then that person draws on the back of the next person, and so on, until the drawing reaches the front person.*
- *The front person reproduces what he or she thinks was drawn on his/her back, then holds up the pencil to show he/she is finished.*
- *As soon as the back person sees the raised pencil, the next part of the illustration is drawn on the back of the person in front, and so on until the entire illustration is reproduced by the person in front.*
- *Remember—no talking. This is not a race; take your time. When everyone's finished we'll see which group is closest to the original drawing.*
- This is an excellent activity for a very differentiated class where some students do not speak the language very well.

Showcase: Showcasing the finished illustrations is a natural conclusion, and is often quite humorous.

* * *

Suggested Designs

- Stick person with some identifying characteristic, such as a briefcase, big hat, or funny hair
- Fish with interesting gills or fins
- Tree with various fruits or flowers on it
- Happy face with unusual eyes, hair, hat, earrings
- Simple animal with some unusual characteristic, such as rabbit with bow, donkey with boots.

Curriculum Connections: Social Studies (ways to meet and greet); Math (simple counting); Science (effects of resistance)

Whole Class

Props: Small paper slips with the numbers 1 through 5 written on them.

117. Shake My Hand

Objective: To locate other members of the class who have the same number as you.

- Divide the class into groups. If your class is divisible by 5, then groups will all have an equal number of students. Otherwise you will need to inform students that some groups have fewer members. Since this is a competitive activity, if you don't let the groups know in advance how many members they have, it becomes an unfair challenge.
- *This game will involve shaking hands with each other, but in a rather unusual way.*

- *Each of you will have a secret number.* Pass out slips of paper, one per student. *Don't show anyone your number. Remember it, then discard the paper slip.*
- *When I give the Start cue, you will walk around the room shaking hands with everyone you meet*
- *But here's the catch. If you had the number 3, then you must pump everyone's hands three times.* Model pumping your hand/arm three times.
- *If you had a 1, pump hands only once. So what will happen when a 1 and a 3 meet?*
  - Model with a student so all can see the resistance offered by the 1 when the 3 tries to continue pumping.)
- *When you have found someone with the same number as you, connect arms and continue to find the other members of you group.*
- *When your group has all its members, quickly sit down on the floor. First group sitting is the winner.*
- This activity can lead nicely into formation of groups for subsequent activity.
- Another way to play this game is to ask students to secretly choose a number between 1 and 5, and then find others who have chosen the same number.

Debrief: Ask students what it felt like when they found someone else with the same number. (It's quite an amazing feeling.)

Extended Debrief: Lengthy discussion about finding someone "just like you" or "not at all like you," or to whatever curriculum connection you may have chosen.

Beyond the Three-Minute Mark

Curriculum Connections: Social Studies (historical information, political platforms); Language Arts (propaganda, bias, elaboration and literary licence in literature)

Whole Class

Prop: A short story with many details

118. Tell It Like It Is

Objective: To repeat a story several times and note the changes in content.

- *For this game, four or five volunteers will wait outside while I tell someone a story.*
- *One at a time, the volunteers will return, listen to the story, then retell it to the next volunteer, until everyone has heard the story.*
- *The last volunteer to hear it must retell it to all of us.*
- This same activity can be done in mime form. The teacher (or a student) mimes an activity (e.g., changing a baby's diaper, changing a tire, making a cake or pizza, looking for lost keys) and the volunteers mime it to each other.
- The short story can deliberately be left unfinished so that it can be used for story completion either by writing, discussing, or illustrating.

Debrief: If the story "morphed" a great deal (which it usually does), discuss the reasons for this. If it came out almost the same, discuss the reasons for this.

Curriculum Connections: Any subject where new vocabulary is introduced; Language Arts (examination of word parts, root words, affixes, word origins, plus close examination and interpretation of nonverbal communication and body language.)

Whole Class

Props: Index cards or slips of paper with unusual words, or new unfamiliar vocabulary from core subjects, printed on one side, with the pronunciation guide and the definitions on the backs of the cards.

119. Sense or Nonsense?

Objective: To determine which of several volunteers is providing the real definition for an unusual and unfamiliar word.

- *This is a word guessing game.*
- *Three volunteers will leave the room with a card that has an unusual word on it.*
- *They will decide which of them will provide you with the real meaning, while the other two will give you false meanings.*
- *You, as a class, will guess who is telling the truth.*
- *This is a challenge—the volunteers against the rest of the class.*
- *We'll guess by a show of hands after all three volunteers have given their meanings.*
  - *If the majority of the class guesses the correct definition, the class wins.*
  - *If the volunteers manage to confuse you, they win.*
- For younger children, it may be helpful to provide three meanings on the card back: one true meaning and two false ones. Older children enjoy creating the false meanings themselves; they soon discover that creating a false meaning based at least partially on some component of the word serves to confuse the class.

Debrief: Ask students what clues the words may have provided to their actual meanings.

* * *

Suggested Words

ULULATE *you-you-late* (to wail or howl loudly)
EFFLUVIUM *ef-floo-vee-um* (an often foul smelling outflow or vapor)
CASTELLATED *cas-tell-ate-ed* having turrets or battlements
ZYMURGY *zee-mur-gee* technological chemistry that deals with the fermentation process, as in brewing
VINEGARROON *vin-i-gar-roon* a large non venomous scorpion like arachnid
TRUNCATE *trun-kate* to shorten by cutting off

Curriculum Connections: Language Arts (close examination and interpretation of nonverbal communication and body language, fact vs. fiction in literature); Social Studies (discussions about the relevancy of news reports, historical events reports, textbook depictions of history; collecting data for research)

Whole Class

120. It's MY Story!

Objective: To determine which of the volunteers is the one that a described story actually happened to.

- *Three volunteers will leave the room for a few minutes.*
- *While there, they must think of something interesting that actually happened to one of them, but they when they return they will each say it happened to them. It is helpful to give a quick example here; e.g., "If Tommy had a bad time at the dentist, Sara would say it happened to her, and Don would say it happened to him."*
- To the volunteers: *You will need to have enough information about the actual event so that two of you can "lie" convincingly. Your job is to fool the class. If the majority of the class chooses the wrong storyteller, you three are the winners.*

- *The class will be allowed to ask each of you questions. You will answer just as if you were the person in the situation. Naturally, for one of you this will be easy; the other two will have to think quickly and try to answer sensibly.*
- While the volunteers are out, prepare the class by telling them to
  - *Watch for nonverbal cues, such as nervous actions.*
  - *Ask questions that will give you good information.*
  - *Ask the same question to more than one volunteer and compare the answers.*
  - *See if the volunteers "trip themselves up" in any way.*
- Bring the volunteers back in and allow about five minutes of class questioning; then vote as to who actually had the experience

Debrief: Ask students what clues may have been given by the volunteers as to whether or not they were telling the truth, and how this information may help them when doing research or collecting data.

Beyond the Three-Minute Mark

Curriculum Connections: Social Studies (exploring careers); Science (the importance of establishing credibility when making generalizations, the importance of asking good questions); Language Arts (related to any literary work where the protagonist is an expert)

Whole Class

Props: Index cards or pieces of paper with professions written on them.

121. The Expert

Objective: To volunteer to become an expert on some silly or ridiculous skill or profession, and be questioned by peers.

- Ask for volunteers. The number will depend on the amount of time you have. A single volunteer can take from two to five minutes.
- Provide index cards for random selection.
- *Please pick a card.*
- *Tell the class what topic you will be an expert in.*
- *Leave the room; you have two minutes to become experts in whatever was on the index card you selected. When you return, we will question you about your new career. You will answer as if you really were that person. You might want to alter the way you stand, talk, or whatever, to seem more like that expert.*
- While the volunteers are out of the room, to the class: *Let's think of how we can ask good questions of them. What sorts of questions might we ask? This is not a guessing game, just a form of entertainment.* Allow students to suggest a few questions. These will flow easily once the interview has begun.
- Bring volunteers back. Be prepared to help with the interview if students get bogged down.

Debrief: After each expert, quickly provide positives about his or her ability to represent.

Extended Debrief: Challenge students to think of more unusual experts. Record these for future games. Invite students to write about an expert of their choice.

*　*　*

Suggested Experts

- Shoemaker for Aladdin
- Toothpick tester
- Artificial-smoke maker for a rock band
- Guitar-string maker
- Felt-pen filler
- Fish gutter
- Chocolate-bar taster
- Lemon squeezer

Curriculum Connections:
Language Arts (learning about adverbs, descriptive writing, verb modifiers); Science/Social Studies (good questioning techniques for research)

Whole Class

122. And the Action Is…

Objective: To guess selected adverbs that are controlling actions performed by peers.

- *This is a game that involves good questioning techniques.*
- *Two volunteers at a time will leave the room.*
- *While outside, they will think of actions to request of the rest of the class.*
- *For example, they might ask someone to stand up or someone else to stretch.*
- *The actions must be the kind that can be easily done.*
- *But here's the catch. When the person does the action, he or she will do it according to the describer—the adverb—we have chosen in the classroom.*
- *It's the volunteers' job to figure out that adverb.*
  - *For example, if the adverb we had chosen was "slowly," then the person would stretch s-l-o-w-l-y.*
- *The volunteers may ask up to five people to do actions before they have to guess. Then they have three guesses.*

Debrief: Discuss what is known about use of adverbs; e.g., most (probably all those chosen) end in –ly.

Extended Debrief: Use adverbs in a writing task.

Curriculum Connections:
Language Arts (learning about propaganda techniques, storytelling); Social Studies (awareness of how history "changes" with retelling)

Whole Class working in Small Groups

Props: Action Cards

Note: No oral communication allowed.

123. Action Telephone

Objective: To pass a message conveyed only through actions, and watch how it changes.

- *For this game, your group will stand in a line, all facing the same direction.*
- Be sure to provide a space for each group.
- *The person at the end of the line will be given an Action Card.*
- *He or she will tap the person in front on the shoulder. That person will turn around and watch as the person acts out whatever is on the card.*
- *The second-last person will then tap the person in front of him or her, and repeat acting out the action, and so on until the front person has received the message.*
- *The front person then acts out the message for the rest of the group to see.*
- *No talking in this game. It's all done by actions.*
- *When your group is finished, sit down on the floor and wait for directions.*
- *This is not a speed challenge. It is a game of communication.*
- Instead of using Action Cards, you can write actions on the board for the "end" persons to see. Then quickly erase these cues.

Showcase: Invite groups to demonstrate their messages by having the front persons show the rest of the class. Discuss how the original message changed (or not).

*   *   *

Suggested Action Cards

- Changing a tire
- Changing a baby's diaper
- Making a cake
- Giving someone a shave and a haircut
- Bathing a big shaggy dog
- Eating ice cream (spaghetti, hot soup)

Index